Dating
for Men

Dating for Men

A GUIDE FOR ATTRACTING WOMEN

PRACTICAL ADVICE FROM A FEMALE DATING COACH

ELSA MORECK

ROCKRIDGE
PRESS

For general information on our other products and services or to obtain technical support, please contact our Customer Care Department within the United States at (866) 744-2665, or outside the United States at (510) 253-0500.

Rockridge Press publishes its books in a variety of electronic and print formats. Some content that appears in print may not be available in electronic books, and vice versa.

Interior and Cover Designer: John Clifford
Art Producer: Megan Baggott
Editor: Brian Sweeting
Production Editor: Mia Moran

Illustrations: SubwayParty/Creative Market. Author photo courtesy of Jake Allen.

ISBN: Print 978-1-64876-099-0 | eBook 978-1-64876-100-3
R0

To my
commitment to
understand the other
side, and to the men
who've lovingly
given me a
chance to.

Contents

Introduction

It's not every day you meet a "Dating Coach." I have one of those job titles that gets people cornered at parties. Yet I suppose the curiosity is warranted: I have the distinct pleasure of helping my clients unearth confidence they never knew they had and take ownership of their love lives. With this book, I hope to help you do the same.

As you probably know already, dating is hard, and for many different reasons. Some of the men I work with aren't sure what they want. Some have just gotten out of a long relationship and discovered that dating is a whole new game now. Others are in their younger years, don't have much experience, and need help building up their confidence. You may or may not be surprised that many of the men I coach are successful by all other societal standards but find women puzzling. All of which is to say, you can be at any stage of your life and still be struggling to develop a lasting relationship.

Certain shifts in our culture have not made this quest any easier. In particular, advents in technology—for example, the ubiquity of dating apps—have made meeting single people in real life relatively uncommon. Our brains just aren't designed to juggle the myriad options presented on apps like Tinder. They've also created a dating public accustomed to novelty—the notion that there's always someone better out there, if only you swipe long enough to find her.

On top of these challenges, the evolution of traditional gender roles and the concurrent rise of a more sex-positive culture has radically changed the way people date. Overwhelmingly, this is a positive thing. But it can be confusing, too. The concept of a "relationship" has become increasingly fluid, and men have been asked to show up differently than they have been for decades. They're expected to learn the language of consent, be more vulnerable, and retire the traditions inherent to the concept of "toxic masculinity." The long-overdue reckoning around sexual harassment and violence, reflected in the #MeToo movement, has forced many men to reevaluate their interactions with women and the underlying power dynamics that govern them. While this work is absolutely necessary, it can have the unintended consequence of making men less inclined to approach or open up to women, for fear of being labeled a "creep"—or worse. Through my coaching, I help men reframe this anxiety as an opportunity: even though the societal scales have been tipped in their favor historically, gender inequities have actually kept men from fully connecting with women and enjoying more satisfying relationships.

Of course, the work I do with clients delves much deeper than dating. I don't believe in merely imparting one-liners and clever pickup tactics, nor do I trade in systems or other manipulative techniques. The best that type of knowledge can do is score you a woman who isn't confident enough to expect better. You don't want that. You want to become the best version of yourself and attract a partner to match.

The purpose of this book is to empower you to become more confident in your own skin and to carry yourself with vigor and passion—to equip you with the foundation you need to attract, engage, and ultimately form real, sustainable connections with women on your own terms. Critically, unlike dating resources for men *by* men, this book offers advice straight from the source. Throughout these pages, you'll not only find my professional advice and wisdom but also relevant testimonials from real women.

Each section of this book builds on the one before it. In part 1, I'll lay the groundwork for dating success, by helping you become the best version of yourself. In part 2, I'll provide practical tips for meeting women, flirting, and becoming more intimate. Finally, in part 3, I'll share insights on entering into an exclusive relationship, as well as how to manage breakups and heartaches.

Some aspects of this book may resonate with you more than others. It goes without saying, however, that the ideas presented herein won't work for you if you don't apply them. It's not enough to know the concepts. You must integrate them into your daily life. I always joke that I offer people who work with me a 300 percent guarantee: what I offer helps 100 percent of the people who do 100 percent of the work 100 percent of the time. The ideas in this book have empowered my clients to push beyond their comfort zones, reach their full potential as purposeful men, and attract their dream women in the process.

So, without further ado, I welcome you on this incredible adventure! Know that as you work through this book, I'm rooting for you every step of the way.

PART 1

THE GROUNDWORK

How do you become the kind of man women want while staying true to yourself? In this opening section, I'll provide some insights to help you answer that question, so you can make the most of the strategies in parts 2 and 3.

1

What Women (Actually) Want

We often think of dating as the way we find love. But the truth is, when you become the best version of yourself, love has no choice but to find you. In this chapter, we'll dispel popular notions about how men should be and demystify what women are *actually* looking for in a potential partner.

THE LIES MEN BELIEVE ABOUT WHAT WOMEN WANT

We're all brought up to believe certain ideas about how we should look, behave, speak, dress, and interact with the opposite sex. So much of what we're taught from a young age fails to align with what we discover about ourselves as we grow older. Though we often consider personal development as *additive*, it may be helpful to reframe your growth as *subtractive*—the process of removing what shouldn't have been there in the first place, in order to reveal the truest version of yourself.

Ask yourself: *what do I think women are looking for in a man*? Regardless of your age, race, or cultural background, it's likely you're thinking of a similar set of traits: an outward projection of strength, both physical and emotional; the ability to assert one's dominance, perhaps by being boisterous or condescending; monetary wealth. Generations of conflicting messages and conditioning, from high school to Hollywood, have polluted the definition of masculinity. As a result, most guys' ideas of what women want are shockingly universal.

But they're not necessarily true, or healthy. When unchecked, these traits can lead to toxic behavior, particularly when it comes to interactions with women. They can also affect you personally: if you are, for example, brought up to believe that sharing your emotions is a sign of weakness, it's only natural that you'd have a hard time opening up to people and forging deeper connections.

In the pages to follow, I've detailed five lies men hear about what women want. The goal here is to question expectations around masculinity in the context of dating, in order to gain a deeper, more nuanced understanding of the kind of attributes women are actually attracted to.

"Women Don't Want a Man Who Shows His Emotions"

Though times are changing, men have traditionally been taught to believe that it's unmanly to express their emotions. Consider the archetypical mid-century American man, solid and stoic, working hard for his family but sharing very little, as if doing so would make him somehow less reliable. Consider the jock standing imperiously atop the high school food chain, wielding his good looks and domineering stature, whose coach chides him to "take it like a man." Consider the heroes men have been told to worship: athletes, world leaders, Hemingway-esque writers. When it comes to men, we are in thrall to courage at the cost of emotional well-being, as if the two can't coexist—which couldn't be further from the truth.

Many men have been denied the tools necessary to articulate and express their emotions. If men don't feel supported in expressing their emotions, they may choose to suppress them, allowing anger and resentments to fester. In personal terms, this suppression can be lonely and isolating. In romantic relationships, it's poisonous. These men may express themselves in unhealthy or even violent ways, lashing out in anger or shutting down completely; they may also construct walls that are impossible for their partners to break through.

The truth is that a man can be strong in character and still display a willingness to share his emotions. In fact, my female clients report feeling closer to their partners when they're emotionally expressive. It may seem obvious, but to create a deep and lasting bond with someone, you have to tell them how you feel! You may have been told "real men don't cry." To the contrary, real men don't hold back when they need to cry.

"Women Want the Man to Take the Lead"

In my work as a dating coach, I often notice a disconnect between what people say they want and what they actually *need* to feel fulfilled. Many women tell me that they want to be in charge. Yet once they achieve this position, some of those same women report feeling less sexually attracted to their partners.

In reality, most couples want an equal distribution of power. But "equal" does not always mean "the same." You may decide where you and your girlfriend are going on vacation, for example, but your girlfriend may take control in the bedroom. In essence, what women really want is not a man who *always* takes the lead by default, but a man who is sure enough of himself to both cede control *and* demand it, depending on what better serves the relationship.

"Women Are Looking For a Provider"

Much like the preceding example, this is a generalized statement that creates distress for anyone who seeks to uphold it, especially in our modern world. With rising costs of living and more women than ever before joining the workforce (at least here in the United States), this notion couldn't be further from the truth. While men are often still the primary breadwinners in some countries, most women would agree that they derive great satisfaction from working and contributing financially to their relationship. What women really find attractive in a "provider" is not necessarily his ability to financially support them, but rather the covetable traits commonly associated with monetary success: ambition, accountability, and a commitment to hard work. An idea better suited to today's world is that women are looking not for men who can provide for them materially, but rather for men who can provide ample love, support, and empathy.

"Women Like 'Macho' Men"

Cue every popular Hollywood flick with the main character who gets the job, the girl, and the social status other men envy. The guy who's emotionally unattainable, loud, and, in some cases, a bully seems to be the one who's constantly winning. But true confidence isn't loud; it's bold.

Fortunately, we're seeing a paradigm shift in modern society. As more men invest in their personal development, the idea of women desiring the loud jock-types seems increasingly outdated. We're learning to value collaboration over competition, friendship over rivalry, and abundance over scarcity. The old paradigm dictated that in order to win, you had to be competitive and outwit your neighbor. The new paradigm is much more expansive; it shows us that by being authentic, we don't need to outwit anyone but ourselves. Creativity bests competitiveness every time. If you're constantly in competition with other men, your growth is limited by theirs. But when you're your own biggest rival, there is no limit. Women aren't looking for men who are loud and competitive. They're looking for men who are focused on forging their own path.

"Women Like Men Who Get With a Lot of Girls"

Years ago, I dated a guy who was obsessed with pickup artistry. Often abbreviated as PUA, pickup artistry has perpetuated the lie that women like men who get with a lot of girls. As hard as it is for me to admit this, I once fell for this lie. This guy actually had me believing that I should thank him for his extensive history of womanizing.

An insidious idea persists, particularly among men but also among women, that the more women a man sleeps with, the more "manly" he is. I have nothing against casual sex, but the idea that men who engage in it should be awarded is foolish. Moreover, the men who sleep with women merely to satisfy a lustful appetite—or secure "another notch on their belt"—tend to be insatiable, because their soul remains hungry for depth. This is, of course, not what women want. Women want a man who has the capacity to attract but the maturity to choose when to indulge his desires—a man who opts for real connections over one-night stands.

Flip the Script: "Nice Guys Finish Last"

As I've told my male clients, there's a difference between being nice and being kind. In my view, niceness stems from a compulsion to appease or please others, whereas kindness comes from an inherent desire to treat others with compassion regardless of who they are or what the reward is. Niceness is easy; kindness is hard. For example, a kind guy might be honest about not wanting to pursue something romantically after a few dates, empowering the woman he's seeing to pursue other people rather than wasting her time. A nice guy might keep things going for fear of hurting this person in the short term, ultimately hurting her more in the long run.

In a sense, nice guys *do* finish last, because their concern for others may be disingenuous, driven by fear or convenience. In my experience, men who prioritize kindness come off as more authentic—and generally more attractive as a result.

THE TRAITS THAT MAKE THE MAN

In the previous section, I challenged outdated notions of masculinity—or, in other words, traits to which most women are not, in fact, attracted. We now have some idea of what women don't want, but what *do* they want? In the section to follow, I'll detail some traits that women actually find attractive in men.

It goes without saying that not all women want the same things and that the traits listed in this section will differ depending on the person exhibiting them. Some of these traits are probably not as intuitive as you'd like them to be—and that's okay. The key here is for you to figure out how to embody these attributes in your own way.

For each trait, I'll share a direct quote from a woman I have coached, so you can see exactly what real women think about men—and what they're looking for in a romantic partner.

Confidence

The number one trait that attracted me to the man I'm dating today is his confidence. From our first date, I could tell he was sure of himself and his direction in life. He didn't preface his sentences or justify his ideas. He expressed himself authentically as someone worth listening to. Despite what the popular myth suggests, you can't "fake it till you make it." Instead, you'd do better to "embrace it till you make it." We're all looking to improve areas of our lives. That doesn't mean you shouldn't be confident in the process. Confidence starts with treating yourself kindly. On our first date, my boyfriend shared his phenomenal weight loss journey and how much it taught him about respecting the promises he makes to himself. Through that journey, he built up his confidence in the gym, which eventually led to having the courage to build his own business. Confidence requires courage because to be confident, we have to bet on ourselves.

"Confidence is a man owning up to his mistakes. I don't expect him to be perfect. I don't expect myself to be, either. So if he makes a mistake, I expect that he owns up to it and tries to make it right if he can."

—*Alyssa, 27*

Vulnerability

There are few things more attractive than a man who's unafraid to share how he feels. For years, boys have been brainwashed to believe that they're weak if they show emotion. But women want you to be vulnerable with them; otherwise, they don't feel like they can truly connect with you. Intentionally sharing your challenges with your partner makes her feel like a valuable part of your life. If it's intimidating to be vulnerable, you can acknowledge that. You can say, "It's really hard for me to be open about things like this, but I want to share the ups and downs with you . . ." and then proceed to share your trials. Love isn't just about celebrating the wins together. It's also about raising each other up during times of hardship. Don't take that opportunity away from her.

REAL TALK

"I like a man who's physically strong and simultaneously isn't afraid to cry in front of me. The fact that I'm the only one who gets to see his vulnerable side makes our connection so special."

—*Rana, 29*

Honesty

One of the common behavioral shifts my clients enjoy after working with me is a newfound ability to speak their minds. Often, they know what to say all along but are too afraid, so they make a habit of speaking circuitously and diluting their thoughts. Consequently, they don't feel heard, and over time it creates distance between themselves and others. Here's the reality: you can't say the wrong thing to the right person. So don't worry about sounding correct all the time. Of course, it's important to be cognizant of the weight of your words, but it's equally important to share the truth. You do a disservice to both yourself and the person you're communicating with when you're not clear. If you want to enjoy dating without wasting time on people who don't want the same things as you, make a practice of being honest.

REAL TALK

"To me, honesty is saying what you need to say. Sure, there's graceful ways to do it, but don't beat around the bush. Just do it."

—*Jane, 36*

Decisiveness

One of the biggest pet peeves my female clients complain about is when men aren't decisive. Far too often, men blow their chances with a woman because they can't take the lead. If a woman asks you what you want to do later that week, don't reply asking her what she's feeling! She's asking you to choose, which is an invitation to take the reins and, frankly, more often than not, a test to see if you will. What sets some men apart is their take-charge attitude. It positions them as men who know what they want, and women love that.

"If you can pick your meal out of a menu in less than five minutes and are pleased with what you get, that's a sign of decisiveness. I hate ambiguity. I like men who know what they want."

—*Maria, 32*

Openness

I was raised in a Middle Eastern culture where it was my dad's way or the highway. I love my father dearly and in recent years have come to understand the culture he came from, but growing up under his rigid rules severely restricted my self-expression. Pulling from those experiences, I knew I had to be with a man who was open-minded and accepting of other perspectives. The premise of this book is to help you grow, so I suspect that by default you're a person who's open to new things. But it's worth mentioning, because a lack of this trait can wreak havoc on a new relationship. Being open simply means that you are willing to hear your partner out and try new things, whether it's going to a marriage counselor or going dancing. Be like water—fluid and adaptable to your environment. That's how you distinguish yourself from other men and keep your connection fresh.

"I'm an adventurous person who likes to break out of her comfort zone. So if I suggest a break-dancing class or escargot for dinner and you're game, then there's a high chance we're gonna work out. Openness to experience is key!"

—*Kelsey, 42*

Self-Awareness

The more self-aware you can be, the more likely you are to be successful with dating. But don't confuse self-awareness with self-deprecation. Self-deprecation is being hard on yourself because you have unchecked insecurities and a warped self-image. Self-awareness is the practice of paying attention to how you interact with the world and making adjustments as needed. It's a judgment-free process that creates room for you to practice intro-spection and reflection. A practical example of this is asking yourself if you've been talking too much on a date and accordingly turning the spotlight back on your company. It might also mean lowering your voice when you realize you're the loudest guy at the bar. The key thing here is to make self-observation a norm in your life so that you're showing up as the best version of yourself.

REAL TALK

"Self-awareness is simple. When we argue, do you have the ability to reflect on it and realize what parts of the argument you contributed to your-self? Being able to see your behavior objectively and course-correct when needed is what keeps relationships alive."

—*Nadine, 28*

Communicative

Of all the things my female clients complain about, this one ranks highest on the list. Most women are more emotionally expressive than are men, and they like to work out their thoughts in dialogue. Society has further supported them in this endeavor. No one raises an eyebrow when a woman talks about how she feels—not so for men. For this reason, conversation can feel sticky when a man and woman first get together.

But this isn't unchangeable. You can learn the skills you need to have effective conversations with your date. First step? Listen better. Learn how to remain present when your date is talking and catch your mind when it wanders. Also pay attention to the *emotion* in what she's saying, more so than the context itself. For example, if she shares that she had a bad day so she decided to go to the park, don't ask about the park! Ask about the bad day she's having. Don't make it your mission to fix her problems. You'll gain far more by simply being a safe space for her to come to when she's upset, rather than trying to fix or change her.

REAL TALK

"I love a man who doesn't hesitate to share what's on his mind and has the vocabulary to articulate it. I hate having to do the heavy lifting. Communicate!"

—*Sharon, 28*

Put In the Work: Reflecting On Your Best (and Worst) Qualities

Try writing out the list of traits from the previous section in a journal, ranking each on a scale of 1 to 5, where 1 indicates a need for improvement and 5 indicates consistent demonstration of the trait. Then reflect on or respond in writing to the following questions.

- **For each trait you scored as a 3 or lower, ask yourself:** What is holding me back from consistently demonstrating this trait, particularly with women? What obstacles are standing in the way? Where might those obstacles have come from? My childhood? The culture at large? Past dating or romantic experiences?
- **For each trait you scored as a 4 or 5, ask yourself:** In which ways do I consistently demonstrate this trait? How does this trait cohere with my overall sense of self? How might I integrate this trait into my approach to dating? How can I use these traits to leverage the ones I ranked lower on?

Naturally, the traits I've described in this section only scratch the surface of what women want. (In my personal and professional experience, other particularly attractive qualities include humor and reliability.) So . . .

- **Reflect on what you would consider your most valuable attributes:** How might you demonstrate these qualities with greater intentionality in a dating context?
- **Reflect on the attributes you'd like to change about yourself:** How might they have gotten in the way of dating- or relationship-related success in the past? How might they continue to get in the way in the future?

One of the most effective ways to change is to begin asking yourself the right questions. The goal of this exercise is to get you in the habit of interrogating the man you are—and highlighting the areas that stand in the way of the man you wish to become.

IT SOUNDS CLICHÉD, BUT . . .

We've talked a lot about what women are looking for in this chapter—so much so that it may feel overwhelming. But as trite as it sounds, women really do just want you to be yourself. Or, rather: the *right* woman really just wants you to be yourself.

Women are intuitive creatures. We can sense when a man is uncomfortable with himself. Are you insecure? Self-conscious? Full of fear? Your energy is contagious. If you want a beautiful woman to feel confident and at ease around you, you have to exhibit confidence and a sense of ease yourself. If you want to see past her physical beauty and appreciate her inner character, you have to see past your flaws and appreciate your own. All too often, I see men who doubt themselves because they don't think they're tall enough, smart enough, interesting enough—the list goes on and on. Some qualities, like your height, are obviously not subject to your control. You can, however, control how you think about these qualities. The moment you decide to love what you've been given, to cherish what makes you unique, is the moment you become a magnet for your dream woman—the person who will love you precisely because you're the person you are.

Of course, some aspects of your personhood may demand deliberate change—some of which I hope this chapter illuminated, and others of which we'll dive into in the next chapter. For a change to be authentic, however, you have to want it first. Contorting yourself to fit some definition of what a woman wants will not propel you toward your happily-ever-after. As you undergo these changes, remember that true confidence comes from the ability to love yourself, even while you continue to make improvements.

Go Forth and Prosper

Takeaways

- Strive for balance in your character. Do the work to unlearn the lies about what women want in a man.
- There is no value gained in putting beautiful women on a pedestal. In fact, this is what beautiful women are used to. When you engage in that type of idolizing behavior, you provoke her to overlook you rather than recognize you as someone worthwhile.
- Embracing and celebrating who you are doesn't mean that you can't grow and change. If there's something you dislike about yourself, you have three options: find the answer inside you; take action; or remain inactive. If it's something you can control, do the work to change it! If it's something you can't change, learn to love and leverage it.

Action Items

- Reflect on or journal about the following questions: What lies about masculinity have made it hard for me to express myself truthfully? Given what I've learned about what traits women are looking for, how will I carry myself with women I'm highly attracted to so I can have a real shot at connecting with them?
- Comedians do a wonderful job at leveraging their "lesser-than" qualities. Take Kevin Hart, for example: He always makes fun of his height. Height is one of the traits that you can't change, and yet Hart still uses it to make people laugh because he's accepted it about himself. People will see you the way you choose to see yourself. Take an hour to watch three 20-minute clips from comedians who don't fit the standard for the "perfect-looking man," and notice how they carry themselves with confidence anyway.
- Make a list of 15 qualities you like about yourself, and place this list where you can see it every day.

Becoming a Man Women Want

Oftentimes, dating feels like a dance between connection and rejection, excitement and fear. It's only natural that our deepest insecurities rise to the surface. The clients I work with are often intelligent, powerful people. But even with all their success, they remain plagued by self-doubt. In this chapter, we'll work on overcoming your limiting beliefs and anxieties in order to bring out the best version of yourself.

PINPOINT YOUR LIMITING BELIEFS

Having been born in the United States and brought up between Japan and Lebanon, with lots of travel to boot, I've been fortunate enough to meet people from a variety of backgrounds. And although the settings may change, when it comes to love, everyone's stories seem to share a theme. That is, limiting beliefs: the constraining ideas we have about ourselves, which hinder our ability to live and love fully. If I've learned anything as a dating coach, it's that success in love is less about overcoming external obstacles and more about simply getting out of one's own way.

Limiting beliefs are not innate. They're learned in childhood, from parents and peers, and solidified throughout our lives. These beliefs pertain to both our physical appearance and our character. They also tend to become self-fulfilling prophecies: if, for example, you believe you're too shy, it may be more difficult for you to muster up the courage to approach women, thus reinforcing the belief that you are, indeed, too shy. And the truth is, until you understand your limiting beliefs, and how they influence the way you interact with others, you will continue to attract people who reinforce those self-perceptions.

Most men I work with struggle with similar limiting beliefs, many of which stem from the ideas about how a man should be, discussed in chapter 1. They include, in no particular order:

- "I'm not tall enough."

- "I'm not interesting enough."

- "I don't make enough money."

- "I'm not cultured or well-traveled enough."

- "I'm not bold enough."

- "I'm not assertive enough."

- "I don't own a house yet."

- "I'm not stylish enough."
- "I'm not fit enough."

Do any of these sound familiar? If so, ask yourself: How and when did I start seeing myself this way? Who told me I was not enough? How has this limiting belief shaped the opportunities I did or did not pursue?

Navigating these questions can be tricky. But the juice is well worth the squeeze. Many of us want to close the gap between how we see ourselves and how the world sees us. But the only way to do that is to confront our limiting beliefs and decide for ourselves how much weight they actually hold. If we're insecure about something that we have the power to change, and that would ultimately lead to greater fulfillment, then we owe it to ourselves to do the work necessary to achieve that change. On the other hand, we must remind ourselves that we are worthy just as we are. For example, if you're on a mission to lose weight and put on muscle, do so from a place of loving your body and being thankful that you have the ability to exercise. Do it from a place of gratitude that you have the resources to eat healthier foods. Looking at it from this angle, losing weight actually becomes a gain, not a loss. In other words, change because you wish to be better, not because you feel you're not good enough.

REAL TALK

"I know I'm a cool person, but all I can think about when I meet a guy I'm super into is: Does my butt look good in these pants? If I add a kissy face emoji in my text, is that too much?! We're all insecure. I just care about making an impression in a city where there's a zillion women for each high-quality guy."

—Natasha, 26

FACE YOUR ROMANCE-RELATED FEAR AND ANXIETY

Fears and anxieties trouble all daters, and for good reason. Fear exists to protect us from harm, while dating demands we make an emotional investment in another person, leaving us exposed to disappointment and heartbreak. I make my living helping people enrich their romantic lives, but even I'm not impervious to these negative feelings.

At their core, fear and anxiety are not injurious to dating. In fact, if you're not at least a little nervous, you're probably not doing it right (or dating the right person). But rather than let fear and anxiety take the reins, it's important to transmute those emotions into something constructive. The Latin root of "emotion" literally means "in motion." It might be helpful to keep this in mind: instead of allowing our negative emotions to paralyze us, we can use them to propel ourselves toward what we want. For example, you may feel intimidated encountering a beautiful woman at the supermarket. Part of you yearns to approach her, but the other part is certain you'll be rejected. What do you do? Many men will think, "Why bother?" and just continue about their day, all the while wondering, "What if?"

But a rare few will answer that question for themselves by moving past their fear and approaching her, potential rejection be damned, allowing their emotions to carry them through their fear and surrender to the unknown. Sure, she may reply coldly or ignore you altogether. But what fun is a life in which you only act in knowledge of a certain outcome?

In the next section, I'll arm you with a few strategies for overcoming your dating-related fears and anxieties.

Embrace the Fear of Rejection

Fear is a natural part of being human—an automatic mechanism alerting us to a threat. While your head knows the difference between the threat of romantic rejection and, say, being chased by a tiger, your body does not. It will do anything to protect you from getting hurt. In the former case, that means instituting a state of paralysis, to prevent you from making your move (in the latter case, that means running, or trying to run, to safety). While it's our tendency to follow our body's natural instincts, we can also work to override that fear in pursuit of goals.

Try to catch yourself in the moment of fear, beating it back with competitive thoughts. If you're feeling paralyzed, for example, you might give yourself a moment to acknowledge it, take a deep breath, and remind yourself, "Sure, she might reject me, but at least I'll know!" If you can alleviate the pressure of trying to control the outcome, you consciously lower the stakes. You'll probably still feel nervous, as you're acting outside of your comfort zone. But at least you will have broken out of your fear.

When you make the transition from dating to a relationship, it's important not to allow your fear of rejection to prevent you from being anything but your authentic self around your partner. It's hard to put yourself out there; when things get serious, your instinct may be to push someone away, put up walls, or deflect. But these alternatives only usher your initial fear into fruition. Worse yet, you'll never know what could've been had you been willing to embrace your fear.

Stop Letting Your Past Become Prologue

One of my favorite quotes is by Dennis Gabor, "The future cannot be predicted, but futures can be invented." It emphasizes human potential and our capacity for reinvention. And yet, that potential is often thwarted by the insecurities hardwired into our brains from past experiences. If you have a history of being rejected, disappointed, or ignored when you approach women, it's only natural to fear approaching women altogether. The same goes for heartbreak: if you've experienced it in the past, your inclination may be to avoid a more serious relationship.

One way to combat this fear is to stay present. It can be easy to base your actions on how you believe women will perceive you. But when you do this, you're denying yourself the pleasure of being in the moment. Instead, approach each new opportunity as a neutral experience. If it works out, you can revel in the results. If it doesn't, you can appreciate the lessons. Remember all that you bring to the table, take a few deep breaths, and approach the situation with no expectations. Celebrate your courage in taking the risk. This is the kind of attitude that inevitably leads to dating success.

Make a conscious decision to distinguish who you are now from who you may have been in previous situations with women. People change! The past does not have to define you. In fact, it may take only one successful approach to convince yourself that you're a confident guy who has the courage to approach women.

Practice, Practice, Practice

It may feel incredibly nerve-wracking to approach a woman in public, or ask her out, or take her on a date. But as with any skill, practice makes perfect. In particular with dating, practice helps you get out of your head; when the experience is no longer new or scary, but rote or quotidian, the same fears and anxieties weighing you down when you first started begin to float away.

The cool thing about modern dating is that approaching women is no longer limited to in-person interactions; you can now approach women online, too—meaning it's easier than ever to get "reps" in (see chapter 3 for more). The not-so-cool thing about modern dating, however, is that so many people rely on dating online that many have forgotten how to exert their social muscles once they're out and about. In order to keep your social muscles in shape, you need to practice! A good place to start is with friends in social settings, like a bar, party, or event focused on a particular hobby of yours. With friends around, you'll have a greater sense of security, which is a good foundation for approaching women.

Know That You're Not Alone

It can be easy to feel like everyone else in the world has dating figured out, while you're destined to a life of singlehood. But having been in this industry for some time now, I can assure you that it's not the case. Even the best daters—the kinds of guys who appear to approach and court women with ease—get rejected and experience heartbreak on occasion, just like everyone else. Humans are built for connection, but in modern dating culture, connection can be hard to come by. I would encourage you to remember that there are so many single people who feel the exact same way you do (and who may be reading these very words at the same moment).

Just knowing you're not alone in how you feel can help you become more patient in, and deliberate about, your dating life. Most of us have been told, in one form or another, that in order to get someone's attention, we have to impress them—tell the funniest joke, bench press the heaviest weight, make the most money. But while impressing people may get their attention, it does not necessarily lead to a healthy and fulfilling relationship. Connecting with people does. Instead of focusing on presenting yourself as the perfect person, give yourself the time to focus on being a real human whom others can relate to—the kind of human who may or may not struggle with dating. This will require vulnerability, which can be scary. But you don't need to disclose your entire life story on the first date to be vulnerable. Simply knowing that it's okay to be honest about your experiences will make you more relatable.

Treat Dating Life like a Lab Experiment

What paralyzes most people in their dating life is attachment to results. What is that girl going to say when I approach her? What if that guy never responds? What if I get hurt again? We place so much emphasis on the outcome that we never go through with the process. The problem is that without the risk, there's simply no reward.

What if you thought of dating not as a gamble but as a lab experiment in which the data was neutral and you learned something valuable no matter the outcome? How much would that open you up to possibility? How empowered would you feel if everything you experienced in your dating life was just that: an experience to learn and grow from and—who knows?—maybe even to enjoy? When you lower the stakes of dating and start to see it as just another activity meant to bring you growth and fulfillment, it alleviates undue pressure on achieving a certain "end." This, in turn, puts you more at ease and positions you as someone abundant and satisfied with who they are, which is half the equation of attracting someone worth your time.

Put In the Work: How Do Your Fears Get In Your Way?

Even the most confident men harbor fears around dating. What are yours? In a journal, rank the following fears on a scale of 1 to 10, where 1 is "not fear-inducing at all" and 10 is "extremely fear-inducing."

1. Approaching women in public.

2. Dating out of your league.

3. Messaging women on social media.

4. Coming up with good ideas for dates.

5. Making the first move on a date.

6. Following up properly after a first date.

7. Maintaining quality conversation on your dates.

8. Sharing vulnerable aspects of your life story with your date.

9. Being yourself around a new person whom you're really attracted to.

Look at your highest-ranking fears and think about how they manifest in your romantic relationships (or lack thereof). How are they preventing you from having a fulfilling love life? What are some steps you can take to overcome them?

Chances are, these fears are keeping you stuck in your comfort zone. The only way to live up to our potential is to challenge ourselves to coexist with and work through our fears. I've seen my clients succeed time and again because they're willing to admit that what they've been doing up to this point hasn't worked—and willing to push themselves to act differently. After all, what is there to lose?

THE BEST OF "YOU"

If the previous sections covered the roadblocks to self-acceptance, this section will help you chart a course to your best, most authentic self. Every man is different. I'm not here to give you one-size-fits-all advice; rather, my hope is to provide you with the motivation, guidance, and ideas to make the kinds of decisions that fit with who you are personally. That may mean eliminating some old habits and committing to new ones; it may mean embracing the values you've always held most dear and giving yourself the space to explore potential forms of self-expression. No matter who the best version of yourself actually is, no matter what the best version of yourself actually does, when you can convey a comfort with your authentic self, the *right* women—the women with whom you're more likely to be compatible—will take notice.

Your Value System

At this point in the chapter, we've talked about limiting beliefs, fears, and anxieties, as well as how to overcome them in your dating life. Now it's time to discuss your value system. Identifying what is and isn't important to you is key to self-acceptance—to owning the person you are and projecting that person into the world with passion and confidence. By pinpointing the kind of man you are, you tacitly identify the kind of woman you *want*.

Among the values on the following list, which ones are most important to you? Are some more flexible than others? Are there others you think you'd like to do a better job of incorporating into your life? Consider these questions, and try writing the answers out in a journal.

Family. How much do you value your family? Do you need them to approve of your lifestyle? Who you date?

Religion. Does religion play a role in your life? Do you belong to a house of worship? How important is it that the person you date shares your beliefs?

Social life. Are you more of a "stay in and watch a movie" or "go out and hit the town" kind of guy? Do you need to hang out with friends frequently? Or are you happy to be with yourself?

Exploration. How important is it for you (and your partner) to lead a life of adventure and exploration?

Political ideals. How important are your political beliefs to your worldview? How important is it that your future partner shares your political views?

Open-mindedness. Do you like trying new things? How accepting are you of beliefs, lifestyles, values, and the like that are different from your own?

Stability. How important is it for you to have stability—emotionally, mentally, and financially? How reliant are you on routines and schedules? Are you capable of living in flux or instability? How spontaneous are you?

Work/life balance. How important is it for you to maintain a healthy work/life balance? Is it important for your partner to have the same balance?

Growth mindset. Do you value learning new things every day? Do you enter arguments wanting to be right or wanting to learn something? Do motivation and ambition come naturally to you, or do they take work?

Humor. How high does humor rank on your list for a romantic partner? How important is it that you laugh together often?

Positivity. Do you usually see the glass as half empty or half full? When conflict arises in your life, do you tend to look for the silver lining or see it as a punishment?

Fitness. What's your relationship with exercise? Do you value a partner who will keep you motivated to prioritize fitness?

Sexuality. How important is it to you that your partner be sexually experienced, or not? How important is it that your partner be willing to try new things in the bedroom?

Now that you've begun to identify your personal values, let's talk about some other areas of your life to consider when building up your 2.0 identity.

Wellness

You've probably asked yourself, *How will I look without my shirt on*? You're certainly not alone. Of course we all want to look our best, but fitness is about more than just looks. It's something you have to work for. It can't be handed down like an inheritance. You have to exert yourself to achieve it and make a decision to maintain it every day. In a sense, that's what makes physical fitness so attractive. It's a sign of discipline and self-respect.

Those qualities of discipline and self-respect underlie all forms of wellness. How do you care for yourself mentally and emotionally? Do you have a mindfulness practice? Do you schedule a weekly dinner with friends or family? Wellness is what *you* do to stay in shape emotionally, mentally, and, yes, physically—not for the sake of vanity, but to maintain your health and project the confidence necessary to attract the kind of women you want.

If you could change one thing about yourself, as it relates to wellness, what would it be? Is it your exercise routine? Your diet? Your stress or anxiety? Once you've decided, ask yourself: what are some realistic steps I can take to improve on this? Consider ways to incorporate solutions into your lifestyle, setting both short- and long-term goals. Hold yourself accountable!

"I just want to feel like my man can protect me if all hell breaks loose. He doesn't need to have a full-blown six-pack, but I do want him to be strong enough to make me feel safe."

—*Ellen, 30*

Style

When it comes down to it, for better or worse, our clothes act as a kind of billboard, making a statement about us before we have a chance to reveal who we are with words and actions. Ask yourself: what do I want my clothes to say about me?

A guy who essentially sticks to a uniform—say, of nice jeans and an ironed black T-shirt—may be tacitly implying that more pressing matters occupy his mental space than what to wear each day. Someone who curates a closet full of expensive suits clearly wants people to know he's wealthy. At both extremes, men have the capacity to attract high-quality women. Most guys fall somewhere in between. The key is to make a choice that works for you and commit to it.

Adhere to similar principles when considering your home decor. Speaking as a woman, few things are more disappointing than liking a guy only to find that his home is a mess. Naturally, the more you care for your home and decorate it to your liking, the more comfortable you'll feel there—and the more comfortable your date will feel there as a result. At the very least, you'll want to make sure your space is clean and inviting, not because girls can't stand a mess—though some can't!—but because of what a mess communicates about you as a potential partner: Are you someone who cares enough about his well-being to clean up after himself? More importantly, are you someone who cares enough about the person you're seeing to clean up for them? You have enough to worry about when you have a girl over. The last thing you want on your mind when you're trying to take the next step in your relationship is whether she's grossed out by your bathroom sink.

Flip the Script: "Peacocking"

As I suggested in the previous section, your style should reflect *you*—it should help deepen and project your authentic self to the women you hope to attract. "Peacocking," a term popularized by the pickup artistry movement, represents the diametric opposite of this. To peacock is to dress or behave in an exceedingly flashy or bois-terous way—say, by sporting a garish pair of pants—in an attempt to outshine other men for female attention. Women pick up on the falsity of peacocking instantly. They might wonder why you can't just relax and be yourself. This isn't to say you shouldn't try wearing bold or adventurous clothing. But if you do, it should be because *you* like it, not for the express purpose of attracting women.

Remember: if you want to be with a catch, you have to be a match! Even if you were to attract a woman by peacocking, she most likely wouldn't be the type of woman this book is aimed at helping you meet. You can't go after a woman who's confident and mature by acting insecure and immature. In general, focus less on competing with other men and more on becoming the best man *you* can be. Men who are comfortable in their own skin display a quiet confidence, which will do more to attract women than any item of clothing would.

Lifestyle

Motivational speaker Jim Rohn famously said, "You are the average of the five people you spend the most time with." This is absolutely true! We acquire the habits and lifestyles of the people we hang out with most often. So it's important to be mindful of our relationships. If your friends do not reflect the man you want to be, it may be time to get new friends. I understand that sounds harsh. But remember, your friends provide your potential partner with a unique glimpse into your life and your discernment of others. She will most likely judge you by your friend circle (just as you would judge her by hers). Moreover, we are usually connected to opportunities through our friends, and we want to make sure those opportunities are worthwhile. If all your friends are homebodies with no ambitions beyond the next episode of some Netflix show, they're not going to be in a great position to help you meet and attract high-value women.

Another aspect of your lifestyle to consider is your extracurricular activities. Most passionate women seek passionate men—that is, men who have a world of their own to excite and inspire them. This world does not necessarily have to be filled with moneyed people or luxury items; it can be filled with literature, or obscure jazz, or uncharted hiking trails. Whatever their passion, these men automatically come across as more confident and self-assured; they're not relying merely on the attention of a woman to galvanize them or give them purpose.

The irony, of course, is that many women want to be a man's center of attention when they know they're not. So when a woman sees that you have passions that are yours and only yours, she feels like she has to work harder for your attention. She may complain about how these extracurricular activities get in the way of your time with her, but secretly she loves how passionate you are about things that have nothing to do with her. When you start to invite her into your world, she'll also feel more special, because she knows what else you could be doing with your time.

REAL TALK

"I don't care about how much money a man makes. I just want to know that once in a while, he'll treat me to something special, and if I feel like packing up and traveling one day, that won't break his pockets."

—*Lara, 46*

Go Forth and Prosper

Takeaways

- Change doesn't happen overnight. But you want your small choices to add up over time. Think about the type of man you want to be 10 years from now. What kind of career path do you want to be on? What do you want people to say about you? What kind of relationship do you want to have, and with what kind of woman? Once you have these answers, you can start to work backward from there, building habits that will help you actualize your vision.
- Everyone has limiting beliefs and insecurities. What distinguishes successful people from failures is how they deal with them.
- Let go of negative thoughts. As soon as one comes up, imagine it passing through and leaving your body. If it feels too hard in the moment to consciously think of anything else, then divert your attention with an activity. Do what you need to do to return to the confident man you are.

Action Items

- If you don't already have one, commit to a workout regimen and a healthy diet that works for you. Choose a friend who can hold you accountable for three weeks until you fully integrate the habit yourself.
- The next time you experience fear of rejection, take five deep breaths in through your nose and out through your mouth. Deep breathing is how we activate our parasympathetic nervous system and disarm our "security system."
- Find a celebrity whose fashion inspires you, and start using them as inspiration to cultivate your personal style.

PART 2

THE FIELDWORK

Now that we've laid the foundation for dating success, it's time to get out there and do the thing! In the next few chapters, I'll provide concrete advice for meeting women (online and in person), flirting, executing a successful date, and, ultimately, taking your relationship to the next level.

Meeting the Women You Want, In Person and Online

Becoming your best self and projecting that self out into the world are not necessarily the same task. The former is a personal process, requiring discipline and consistency, whereas the latter requires a degree of social and emotional intelligence. In this chapter, I'll help you discover what you're really looking for when it comes to dating—and learn how to bring your best self to bear in order to get it.

FIRST THINGS FIRST: WHAT ARE YOU LOOKING FOR?

As we discussed in chapter 1, women find assertive men incredibly attractive. But for a man to be assertive, he has to know what he wants.

You'd be surprised how few men actually take the time to set their intentions. If you're like most people—including me, once upon a time—then you probably date passively. You go out with the goal of meeting people you're attracted to, without giving too much thought to what might happen after that.

While dating in this manner can seem natural, it doesn't lead to long-term success. You may end up hurting someone you like by leading them on. Conversely, if you're not clear about your expectations, you might expose yourself to disappointment. Far too common is the guy who says he's "up for anything," only to find his heart broken when the girl he's seeing casually mentions she's also been seeing someone else. Far rarer is the guy who has enough confidence to be honest with himself and the girl he's seeing—to move past the games and tell her what he really wants.

So before you get out there, ask yourself: What are you *really* looking for right now? A serious relationship? Something more casual? To simply experience whatever the dating world has to offer after a long-term relationship or divorce? If your dating experience is limited, you may need time to explore—to learn more about yourself and what it is you're really looking for in a long-term partner. Consider your values from the previous chapter: at present, what kind of relationship would best complement them?

To be clear, you don't *need* to want a serious relationship. As long as you're clear about your intentions from the get-go, you'll be golden. If my female clients are any indication, this clarity will be met with relief. And remember: love is as much about timing as it is about anything else. Even if you're not ready for it right now, trust that it will find you when you are.

REAL TALK

"I've learned to stop dating men who reply to my questions with vague answers, or worse, more questions. Decisiveness is key. Know what you want before you start entangling people in your confusion."

—Monica, 32

Put In the Work: Determine Your Criteria

My mother always told me, "If you don't know what you're looking for, you'll never know when you've found it." She was referring to my career path, but it's no different in dating.

This is why I have my clients create Ideal Partner Criteria. To begin, write down everything you're looking for in a person. At this point, you should've already asked yourself what type of relationship you want, so you don't need to include that. Instead, focus on character traits and values that are important to you (referring back to the work you did in part 1). Once you have this list, choose three absolute non-negotiables that must be present for you to even consider dating this person. Just three! For some, pickiness is a cop-out—it can give you an excuse to not put yourself out there in the first place.

Challenge yourself to really think about what's important to you. Personally, my list for a partner was:

- 29 years old or older
- Supportive
- Generous

That's it. Though it was incredibly tough to narrow down my list to three traits, I honored it in my search. When I met my current partner, his physical attractiveness wasn't what captivated me—not at first. Of course I thought he was handsome, but it wasn't what made him stand out to me. In fact, I never thought I would date a bald guy, and while our first date was amazing, it definitely wasn't love at first sight. Had I been overly selective, I may never have given him a chance. Instead, I chose to be flexible and allow our connection an opportunity to develop. To my delight, I fell deeply in love with him and, in time, found him to be one of the most handsome men I've ever met.

HOW TO MEET WOMEN IN REAL LIFE

Meeting someone you align with intellectually, emotionally, sexually, recreationally, and spiritually can be incredibly difficult—especially in today's world. For starters, the dating scene has almost completely moved online. Whereas in the past we had no choice but to meet our partners at work, in bars, in houses of worship, or wherever else we spent time in our community, myriad dating sites and apps have done their best to render real-life approaches irrelevant. Or, if not irrelevant, weird. Indeed, simply making eye contact with a stranger feels out of the ordinary. In the past, a situation as simple as getting into an elevator with a stranger served as an opportunity for conversation. But today, we're saddled with a permanent social crutch: the smartphone. Not only does it frequently preclude our need to socialize, it ends up consuming much of our attention when we do.

But all hope is not lost for meeting women IRL. Provided you know what you're looking for, there are still opportunities in your everyday life to meet women. I've broken down a few in the pages to follow.

Through Friends

The Situation: Meeting a potential date through friends is by far one of the most effective strategies. Birds of a feather flock together, and when it comes to who you date, it's no surprise that someone who gets along with your friends will probably get along with you. So tuning in to your friends' networks can be an awesome way to connect with women. Remember that like attracts like, so if you're already in a setting that you and your friends enjoy, the probability for success is higher.

The Approach: Be upfront. I recommend letting your friends know that you're interested in meeting someone. However, it's critical to only ask people who really understand your taste. One of your friends' girlfriends would be ideal, as women are typically more intuitive when it comes to setups. Once they have someone in mind, they can arrange an organic setting for you to meet. A dinner party or an intimate gathering, such as a game night, is best (in general, you don't want to have to shout to hear each other). Unless the friend who's setting you up isn't someone you see regularly, you don't want, or need, to go right into a date setting. Something more informal gives you both a chance to see if a date is something you're interested in.

MAKE YOUR MOVE

You're at a low-key gathering with your friends, along with the cute friend of your friend. Things are going well. And you notice, every so often, that said cute friend is looking your way, trying to catch your eye. But how do you take it to the next level?

Rather than ask her out there and then, relieve yourself of the pressure to make a move or ask for her number. Just enjoy the gathering for what it is. The next day, catch up with your friend and ask them how they thought it went, and have them find out if the cute friend might be willing to give you her number. This gives her the space to decide on her own terms whether she really wants to see you, without putting her on the spot in a group setting.

The Workplace

The Situation: Using the workplace as a means of meeting a love interest is tricky. But if executed appropriately, it can prove successful. Countless relationships and marriages—but also breakups and affairs—begin in the tight quarters of the office.

The good news is, the people you work with already have at least one thing in common with you: they chose to work there. But there are other factors to consider before you make a move on one of your coworkers—namely, the power dynamics at play. Making a move on a subordinate, for example, is almost always a bad idea, as they may feel professionally pressured to say yes. (If you're interested in a superior, you'd similarly want to consider the impact it could have on your job.)

All things considered, there's nothing inherently wrong with meeting women in the workplace. We spend most of our lives working and make many genuine friends at our offices, so it's only natural that some of the professional relationships we cultivate have the potential to turn into something more.

The Approach: Because of these dynamics, you probably want to make sure this coworker is on the same level as you—or, better yet, in a different department altogether—before considering them as a potential date. The last thing you want to do is overstep your boundaries or make someone feel uncomfortable, even if that wasn't your intention. Another factor to consider is the social dynamic of the workplace. People are more or less paid to be friendly at work, so it takes an added level of discernment to distinguish a regular interaction from a flirtatious one (see chapter 4 for more on flirting).

Refrain from flirting or trying to develop a connection before you have ample evidence that it's the right time. Given the politics of the workplace, stick to benign compliments about what she's done (e.g., "Great job on the project") or what she's wearing (e.g., "Are those new shoes? They're awesome"), as opposed to more overt compliments (e.g., "Wow, you look beautiful"). Don't go out of your way to endear yourself to her. Just be yourself and see how she responds. Look for cues like sustained eye contact, excessive laughter, light touching, and other nonverbal indicators of attraction. Even then, pay close attention to the content of your conversations: Do they just involve work? Have you discussed each other's personal life? Is she definitely single and open to a connection at this point in her life? Before you think about making a move, it's key to make sure you've established a *personal* relationship independent of your *working* relationship.

MAKE YOUR MOVE

Fortunately, many workplaces provide opportunities for coworkers to get together outside of the office. Rather than ask someone out at the office, attend organized team outings, happy hours, or other events. Getting to know this person outside the office can help you both let your guards down and be yourselves.

If she shows interest, start with something casual—perhaps a coffee before work or drinks on a Friday. Should this activity go well, clarify your intentions, albeit gently: you want to make sure she knows you're interested in something more, but you don't want to make her feel uncomfortable if she's not on the same page.

The Bar, Party, or Event

The Situation: Another great place to scout for dates is in a public setting such as a bar, party, or event, like a street festival or convention. Historically, bars have gotten a bad reputation, but much like any other situation, it depends on what you make of it. Bars, events, and parties are great opportunities to meet women because the ambience is already set for you. Generally, people are there to meet other people and have a good time. All you have to do is show up looking sharp and ready to flex your social muscles.

The Approach: For social settings with large groups of people, the key is to read the room early on so you know where to invest your energy. Your eye will naturally gravitate toward the women you find most attractive. But it's not enough to find a woman attractive. If you try to pull every beautiful girl you see, you'll come off as desperate.

As I've said before, women are intuitive creatures. We can tell by the way you approach whether you're just there to get laid or you have a real interest in getting to know us. If you want a woman's full attention, you have to be willing to give yours first, so focus less on the result (e.g., getting her phone number) and more on the moment (e.g., having an interesting conversation).

Before you make your move, try initiating eye contact or eliciting a smile to gauge her interest. If she's with a group of friends, then you have to be more strategic. Make sure there's been enough back-and-forth eye contact and acknowledgment on her end before walking up to her. Ideally, you'll want to find a moment when she's separating from the group, perhaps to head to the bar for another drink. Another idea is purchasing her a refill of what she's drinking. That will get her attention and encourage her to walk away from the group to talk to you. Keep in mind that what you say is less important than how you make her feel. In other words, you could literally walk up to her and make a comment about her shoes, but if it comes off as genuine, it will be far more effective than a clever one-liner.

Flip the Script: Conversation Starters

For as long as men have been picking up women at bars, there have been generic pickup lines, delivered by slick, faux-confident guys with no real interest in the girls they talk to. Think: "Come here often?" or "Did it hurt? . . . When you fell from heaven?" The reason these pickup lines don't work on (most) women is the same reason so many of us hate commercials: they're trying way too hard to sell you something you probably don't want in the first place. Not only have most women heard them all before, they'll immediately categorize you as a desperate man with no real depth.

Naturally, opening up a conversation with a woman is scary! So it's understandable that you'd want to resort to well-trod tactics. But instead of trying to sound clever, focus on being real and connecting with them. The most organic way to start a conversation with a woman is to do just that. "But what do I talk about?" you might ask. The truth is, if you're truly present in your environment, tuned in to the moment, and genuinely interested in the person you're speaking with, you're much less likely to run out of things to say. You might comment on the music, her shoes, or maybe even the DJ's weird haircut. Don't overthink it. If all else fails, just introduce yourself and ask her name.

The best way to soothe an overactive mind is to act. Once you make your move, you'll be forced into the moment. And from there, so long as you're paying attention, you'll know what to do.

Sites of Mutual Interest

The Situation: If you love going to museums, chances are the museum is a good place to meet women who do, too. If you love playing basketball or soccer, a good place to meet women who share those interests is in local (coed) intramural leagues. Investing in your hobbies and passions is not only a great way to develop new skills and add flavor to your life but also an opportunity to meet women with whom you already have things in common.

The Approach: Just because you can make a move on women doing what you love doesn't mean you should. Women don't necessarily want to be approached when they're partaking in their hobbies. I've heard many women complain about men approaching them at the gym, because that time is meant for them to indulge in some much-needed self-care. In short, they're not there to meet guys, they're there to work out! So you need to be strategic about making your move. The best way to do that is to approach the situation as if you were just looking to make some new friends who enjoy doing the same activities as you. Free yourself from any outcome beyond that. This will alleviate any pressure to perform on your end, and will make women more comfortable around you.

MAKE YOUR MOVE

> The great thing about approaching a woman in a site of mutual interest is that talking points are readily available. Make the conversation about the topic you're interested in, while looking for the kind of cues discussed in the previous section. If she seems interested, casually asking her to do something that involves your interest is a safe bet. (If, for example, you do meet at the gym, maybe there's a class you can both take.) At this point, it's not about "going on a date"—it's simply about continuing to connect over something you both love. This builds rapport and takes the edge off going out with a stranger.

Neighborhood Restaurants, Cafés, and Other Local Spots

The Situation: The hospitality industry is known for employing attractive women. Whether it be restaurants, lounges, or cafés, there's usually no shortage of women who might make a great date. But women who work in this industry in particular are paid to be polite. And the female regulars are likely not there to meet men.

The Approach: It's your responsibility not to conflate someone's job (like the overeager politeness of a server) with romantic interest. The key here is to put the ball in her court. Whether she's your server at a restaurant, the desk clerk at your local bookstore, or the cute girl working away on her laptop at your favorite café, it's important to not make her feel awkward while she's on the job (or simply working). Furthermore, you must be ready to never return to that place again, *especially* if she works there; if you continue to frequent her place of work after making her feel uncomfortable, it's tantamount to harassment.

> ## MAKE YOUR MOVE
>
> If you're ready to risk severing your ties with your neighborhood spot, focus on building a genuine connection first. Compliment her on the way she's doing her job, but not in a sleazy or corny way. If she's been timely with your food, let her know. You can ask a few personal questions in the interaction, but don't go too deep. Remember that you want to keep the interaction lighthearted, because she's still at work. Assuming you've had a pleasant and reciprocal interaction, the move is to simply leave

her your number on your receipt or a piece of paper. This gives her all the power: she can either call you or not. It also positions you as a confident guy detached from the outcome: if she calls you, great; if not, no sweat.

HOW TO MEET WOMEN ONLINE

Men and women alike tend to loathe dating apps. Originally created as a means of meeting a spouse, they've since evolved into romance's equivalent of fast food. While they may expand your dating pool, profiles only offer the cardboard cutout version of a flesh-and-blood person, culling a few select photos and attributes from the three-dimensional man you are. You might miss out on someone great simply because they failed to represent themselves well on an app. Conversely, with some clever photography—and nobody to hold them accountable for telling the truth about their lives—the chances you meet someone who doesn't turn out to be as awesome as they appear are still quite high. That's not to say there aren't genuinely good people on dating apps looking for a meaningful connection: according to a 2019 Pew Research Center report on online dating, 12 percent of US adults have found a committed relationship through a dating app or website.

Everyone wants to recount the story of meeting their future spouse in line at the deli counter or traipsing the rows of a used bookstore. But in the real world, these "meet-cutes" don't always happen. When discussing online dating with my clients, I try to get a sense of their lifestyle and whether they've had success with apps in the past. I recommend them more often to introverted clients than extroverted ones, but it all depends. The fact of the matter is, a dating app is simply a tool. And much like a hammer, its efficacy relies on proper application.

The Sites and Apps

There are a multitude of options, and the one (or few) you settle on ultimately depends on different factors, such as where you live, how old you are, and what you're looking for out of dating.

Generally speaking, if you're above the age of 45 and searching for a serious commitment, great platforms to use are Zoosk, OkCupid, Match, or even OurTime, whose user base mainly consists of people over 50. If you're 45 or younger and live in a metropolitan area like New York City, Chicago, or Los Angeles, Hinge is great for finding a more meaningful connection. Hinge lets you know exactly what part of your profile a match specifically liked. For example, if you have a picture that was taken in Japan, someone can like that specific picture, organically kicking off a conversation about a mutually interesting topic.

Among all the apps mentioned, Tinder continues to reign supreme in terms of popularity and usage (particularly if you're outside a major metropolitan area or not in the United States). So while swiping may take longer because of all the choices, probability-wise, you have a solid chance of meeting someone. It'll simply require more patience and intentionality. Given the minimal effort required to really use the app, you shouldn't always expect timely responses or serious conversations. And because you're evaluating people almost entirely based on their looks, you're liable to forge shallower connections.

MAKE YOUR MOVE

When you want to transition from the dating app to a real-world date, the most important thing to remember is to focus less on impressing and more on connecting. Reciprocation is a must. This is where so many people mess up on dating apps. They engage in small talk or offer one-word responses, which simply don't generate enough back-and-forth for a connection to develop. When you're interested in moving things offline with your match, make sure that you're ready to listen (even if you're just reading words on a screen) and to respond invitingly so that she feels like she's connecting with a real human. You might do this by asking her things about her personality and moving beyond the mundane topics of what she does for a living or how her week has been. Instead, try asking what the most exciting part of her week has been. Ask her how adventurous she is on a scale of 1 to 10. Ask her what her favorite childhood memory is.

But remember: don't get into the habit of turning your crushes into pen pals. The phone is for logistics; the date is for getting to know each other.

Social Media

Similar to dating sites and apps, social media is another great way to connect with people online. And unlike the former, social media can be more personable if done the right way. Since a social media profile shows you a more extensive timeline of the person you're approaching, you have more potential talking points. Furthermore, you can go through your existing network on Facebook or Instagram, essentially using it as a vehicle to meet people through friends or acquaintances. If you've met someone in person, connecting on social media is a great way to deepen a connection in a neutral context, by sending each other relevant posts or commenting on each other's pictures.

That said, attractive women are constantly inundated with men trying to hit on them on social media. And since social media is not expressly intended for dating, you have to be careful with how you go about using it for that purpose.

IF YOU'RE USING FACEBOOK

You'll want to focus on people with whom you have mutual friends. Ideally, you'll want to add the person you plan to message as a friend first so that your message has a higher chance of actually being seen, and because it builds better rapport if they've accepted your request before you reach out. From there, you can go ahead and send a quick message letting her know the intent behind the friend request. If you notice a theme running through her profile, make note of it and add it to your initial message. Your goal is to meet up because she's attractive and seems cool, right? Find a middle ground between making your intentions clear and not being too forward. That might look like mentioning something interesting you found in one of her pictures. (Maybe she rescues pit bulls? Maybe she just got back from Hawaii? Maybe she plays soccer?) Then tie that into the message. Let her know it stood out to you and that, if you had to guess, she strikes you as an adventurous (or another positive adjective that seems relevant) woman. From there, it should be easy to steer the conversation in the direction of meeting up.

Finally, don't be disappointed if she says no. Meeting up with strangers from the Internet is scary, and it's not something all women are into. If that ends up being the case, let her know it was nice to meet her and move on. If she does want to meet, make sure you choose somewhere public and keep it casual.

IF YOU'RE USING INSTAGRAM

The same rules apply for those in your social network. If, however, you plan to use Instagram as a means of messaging women you're not connected with, a good strategy is to use the geotag feature.

Most people tag the location of their pictures, so this is a shortcut to finding women in your vicinity. Once you've started browsing through profiles of women in your location, the next step is to be intentional about *who* you message. Far too many men aimlessly message women without putting thought into what they're saying or who they're talking to. Women can sense this, and even if your clever attempt works at first, you'll eventually be found out.

Spend some time on her profile to learn things about her personality. While her looks might be the first thing you noticed about her, it's important to see her as a whole person. Since Instagram stories are created in real time and are less curated than regular posts, they make room for a conversation about something that's immediately relevant to her life!

Some examples of things you can message her about: places she's traveled that you've been to yourself; the food she posts pictures of; her pet; her hobbies; or anything else that pertains to her unique personality. The best way to start out your message is with a genuine compliment about her personality or account; the best way to end it is with a question. You'll also want to make sure that you have enough activity on your profile to make her feel comfortable messaging back. If you only have a few posts and barely any followers, you might come off as a creep—that is, someone who's only using Instagram to pick up women.

Put In the Work: An Insider's Guide to Building a Dating Profile

There are two central questions you should have in mind when building a dating profile: Who is my best self? And how do I portray him in this format?

Portraying your best self is not the same as seeking to impress women. Rather, you want to showcase your multifaceted personality in a way that makes you seem interesting and approachable. Given the limited space available, you want to sum yourself up neatly. Remember: you only get out what you put into these apps, so if who you put in is someone else entirely, it's unlikely you'll find someone you're actually interested in.

To help point you in the right direction, I've provided this handy list of Dos and Don'ts.

DO: Include pictures of you doing what you love. Think hobbies, places you've traveled, or simply spending time with family and friends (or, of course, your beloved pet).

DON'T: Include mirror selfies, pictures of yourself at the gym (even if that's an activity you love), or pictures of yourself in the bathroom. Period.

DO: Include pictures from several angles. As anyone who uses dating apps knows, pictures can be deceiving. So it's best to get pictures of you from different angles so she gets an accurate depiction of you. The last thing you want is for her to feel tricked (or disappointed) when she sees you in person!

DON'T: Include pictures of you flexing your muscles. No matter how big they are, it just comes off as shallow and sleazy.

DO: Fill out your profile in its entirety. You want to narrow your search to the women you can develop a deeper connection with; the more of your personality you project, the more likely you'll match with someone who shares your interests and values.

DON'T: Make self-deprecating remarks about yourself in your profile. You might think it's funny or humble to do so, but it can be perceived as a sign of insecurity. Much like with a job résumé, you want to put your best foot forward on an app!

DO: State what you're looking for. Profiles with the most clarity have the greatest success. Take the time to share what you're looking for in a potential partner to increase your chances of matching with the right women.

DON'T: State what you're *not* looking for. While it seems like a good idea to be explicit about what you don't want, this can end up back-firing by casting you as overly picky.

DO: Be cognizant of your body language in your pictures. Tiny adjustments like good posture, keeping your hands out of your pockets, and smiling in your pictures can go a long way in securing a woman's attention.

DON'T: Only post formal or casual pictures of yourself. Mix it up! Have a picture of you in a suit and another one of you in swim shorts or athletic wear.

DO: Highlight your personality and quirks. What are the things that make you unique?

DON'T: Make your bio feel like a résumé or standup routine. Focus on the parts of your personality that you can share with another person, not those that will secure you a job. And don't put too much pressure on yourself to come off as hilarious to catch someone's eye. You want this person to take you seriously as a potential mate (and to save your best stuff for when you meet in person, anyway).

"My favorite profiles of men are those that have enough writing in their bio for me to start a conversation with them, and enough pictures from different angles so I know what I'm working with."

—Jessabelle, 26

HANDLING REJECTION

Everything outlined in this chapter is designed to help set you up for dating success, but that doesn't mean that rejection won't be part of the process. In fact, rejection will more than likely be a substantial part of it. If you play to win, the risk of losing is always there.

Of course rejection sucks. It can even make you angry, spiteful, or pessimistic in future interactions with women, especially if it keeps happening over and over again. This is not a useful response. Instead, allow yourself to react, but once those intense feelings subside, remember to have empathy for the person who's doled out the rejection. Being sensitive to someone else's experience—particularly all the facets of their experience you cannot see—will make the rejection feel less personal.

If you let it, rejection can be a transformative experience. When someone pushes us away from them, they tend to push us closer to ourselves. We grow more curious when we've been rejected, even if the curiosity forces us to ask questions we might have avoided in the past. We become more sensitive to our environment, more aware of the possibilities. Sometimes, it has an adverse effect of making us more rigid and unavailable, but that's a defensive, protective posture.

Few moments in life have the capacity to redirect us like rejection. Whether it's in a career or a relationship, it fuels us with a deep need for change. I ended up in Austin, Texas, because of a failed love story.

Looking back at it now, I can't imagine any outcome that fits me as well. But you never see that in the moment. No's light fires under us. They force us to look inward. Thank rejection when it slams the door in your face. Bow to it and kiss the doorknob, because I promise it'll all make sense when you take a few steps in another direction.

Go Forth and Prosper

Takeaways

- Capitalize on everyday moments to meet women. Be bold but tactful in your approach.
- When you get a girl's number, wait up to 48 hours to text, but no longer than that. I know the infamous rule here is three days, but the reality is, a woman who knows her worth doesn't want to play games. If you're interested in her, let her know before she moves on to the next guy. Keep the text short and sweet, and refer to something specific in your interaction to reignite the bond. From there, the next goal is to set up a date as soon as possible.
- True confidence is the ability to reassure yourself that you'll be fine no matter what happens. It's that level of self-love that's going to allow you to take the risks that are necessary to find true satisfaction in your love life.

Action Items

- Approach three women in person over the next week. Focus on striking up a conversation and making a connection, however weak or fleeting. If you get a number, great!
- Download the dating app(s) you plan to use, and start building your profile based on the tips in this chapter. If you already have a profile, spruce it up with the tips shared here.
- Find eight women in your existing social media network that you find attractive and who appear to be single, and message them something relevant about their profile.

Flirtation and First Dates

Congratulations! You scored a first date. Now it's time to make a lasting impression. In this chapter, I'll help you plan and execute a great first date, up your flirting game, and, hopefully, secure a second date. No matter the outcome, this is the most exciting part of the process.

THE INSIDER'S GUIDE TO A GREAT FIRST DATE

First dates can be scary. After all, it's the first time this person, perhaps a total stranger, is evaluating you as a potential partner. You're putting yourself out there, exposing yourself to possible rejection. But remember: as nervous as you are, your date is probably feeling the same way.

To mitigate the nerves, scale back your objective. Don't go into the date thinking you have to fall in love before the first course arrives. Don't go into the date with the goal of sleeping with her—or even kissing her. Simply head into the date with this goal: to assess whether the connection warrants another date.

Keep your plans relatively simple. The agenda is for you two to get to know each other better, so you don't want to pick somewhere crazy loud. Nor do you necessarily want to choose a formal setting, where the pressure for it to go well is higher. A cozy café, neighborhood tavern, or park is far better suited to casual conversation. If you have the option, I recommend sitting at the bar versus getting a table, which creates more distance between the two of you. (If you do get a table, try to sit next to her rather than across from her.)

Of course, you also want to match the date to the girl you're taking out. Based on what you know about her, you can ask some leading questions to confirm you're heading in the right direction (e.g., "Are you more of a wine or beer person?"). While she can definitely help you come up with date ideas, you should be the one leading this first interaction. Even the most empowered women like knowing that the man they're with can take charge, and the first date is your opportunity to do just that!

If you want to add a little more spice to this process, make the interaction fun from the get-go. Rather than ask her how her week is going as a preface to the date, try asking her something more compelling, like: "On a scale of one to ten, how adventurous are you?" Based on her answer, you can come up with something a bit more outside the box! This could be an outdoor activity, or something as simple as packing a picnic basket and finding a nice place to hike.

Here are a few frequently asked questions about first dates, answered:

How many activities should I plan? Ideally one or two activities is best. You can do a game night over drinks or a coffee and walk around the city—something a bit more active is a great way to cut through the initial nerves. That said, you don't want to hold your date too long. It's best to leave some mystery for future dates.

How should I respond if she offers to pay? Let her know it's your treat, and that you're happy she came out, then thank her for offering. If she insists, let her know there will be another opportunity for her to treat you. Some women won't admit it, but they love it when a man cheerfully pays for the first date. Even though we live in the modern world, it's wise to take what we love from the past along with us.

Is it a bad sign if we don't kiss on the first date? Contrary to popular belief, it's not the end of the world if you don't kiss on the first date. We've been taught over and over again that a kiss must happen at the end of a good date. But sometimes it takes longer than that to warm up to a new person, and not all women place that pressure on themselves. Worry less about getting the first kiss and focus more on having a good time and creating the best experience you can for your date.

Should we have sex on the first date? Generally speaking, I advise against sex on the first date. In my experience, it's best to build up the sexual tension and release it only when the emotional connection has been solidified. Obviously, this all depends on your dating goals. If it's to land a girlfriend, I'd recommend holding off on sex the first time you meet. Sex can unnecessarily complicate things.

What are some first date no-no's? Don't be on your phone while you're together. Turn off your dating app notifications. Stay away from politics and religion. Don't self-deprecate. Don't forget to compliment and flirt with her.

Should it just be us on the first date? Traditionally speaking, we all think of dates as an experience shared between two people. But if it just so happens that she's out with friends and invites you, or vice versa, it's not a deal breaker. On the contrary, first dates spent with friends can get you their approval right away before you put effort into planning a second date.

Put In the Work: The First Date Checklist

Try reviewing this checklist before your next first date. Some of the points may feel like common sense to you, but they're still helpful to keep in mind!

☐ **Wear an outfit you feel confident in.** You don't want to be someone you're not by wearing something out of character, but you do want to look your best. Put on your favorite watch or wear your go-to cologne (but not too much!).

☐ **Come prepared.** You want to have a sense of the place you're going. For example: Is there a part of the bar or restaurant that's too loud or crowded? What kind of seating do they have? If you're eating, what's the food menu like? How casually do people tend to dress there? You don't have to make a full recon mission out of it, but you don't want any unpleasant surprises.

☐ **Show up a few minutes early.** This gives you a chance to find a seat or secure a table, so you don't have to negotiate that during the first few minutes of the date.

☐ **Compliment her upon greeting each other.** Your date put in effort to look good for you. Take a moment to let her know! Be sure to make your compliment authentic.

☐ **Remember to listen more than you speak.** There are different levels of listening. Listen with the intent to learn, not to respond. Ask her questions and listen carefully for the emotion in her answers. You'll get bonus points for pointing out the emotion you pick up on!

☐ **Make a mental note to avoid controversial topics.** As passionate as you might be about politics or other hot-button issues, a first date is not the time to hash them out.

THE FINE ART OF FLIRTATION

There's a fine line between platonic and romantic. What separates the two is the presence of sexual chemistry. Flirting is a great way to suss out whether this chemistry exists. Flirting is difficult for many men, especially inexperienced daters. Even the smallest flirtations amount to a leap of faith—in a sense, what you're doing is tacitly communicating interest in someone (oftentimes, sexual interest). It's a vulnerable position to put yourself in, leaving you open to rejection. And while it comes naturally to some, many men don't really know how to flirt—or what constitutes flirting in the first place—thus making them liable to end up in the "friend zone" with someone they really like (see chapter 6, page 105).

Typically, I tell my clients to think of flirting as a playful challenge. You want to challenge your date, but not in a way that will threaten the rapport or make them uncomfortable. To reiterate, even when flirting, focus less on impressing and more on connecting! There is no one-size-fits-all approach to flirting, because flirtation should be unique to you—and the person you're flirting with. When you approach your dates from this angle, you lower the stakes, which makes it easier to be authentic.

Flirtation is not limited to verbal exchanges. I would encourage you to wait for your date to initiate touch before you attempt to flirt physically. Until you get that invitation, find opportunities in conversation to lightly challenge your date. Maybe push back on some of her ideas that you don't agree with, or ask her how she came to those conclusions. No one has died from a little challenge! In fact, it's perfectly healthy for you not to agree with everything she says, and it's a mark of confidence to be able to make that apparent.

Still, too much of a good thing can be a bad thing, and flirting is no exception. So mix up the playful banter with regular conversation, to make sure you're connecting on a deeper level. And remember: Flirting is not putting down or shaming the other person. Flirting isn't starting a political debate with your date. Flirting isn't overpowering or talking down to your date. Flirting isn't nonconsensual touch or vulgar commentary. When in doubt, leave it out! And keep reading for some more specific guidance . . .

Speak with Your Body Language

I probably don't have to tell you that a majority of human communication is nonverbal. In few situations is this more important than between humans who are romantically inclined toward each other.

Pay attention to the cues your date is giving you here. Body language is a kind of dance, and you don't want to move out of step with your partner. You might start by trying to catch her eye over conversation, prolonging the eye contact until it forces a smile. If she looks away or seems uncomfortable, turn away.

If a woman is open to introducing more proximity, she may brush her arm against you, graze your knee with hers, casually scoot her chair closer to yours, or lean in when she talks. You might respond in kind, by touching her shoulder or knee when you make a joke, gauging her comfort level, and then leaving it be if she seems receptive. The key is to gain consent with every new touch—if she, for example, moves her knee away at the touch of your hand, don't try to touch her knee again until she initiates closer proximity.

By the end of the date, you may catch her looking at your lips, which is another way of saying she wants to kiss you. That said, I don't recommend rushing the first kiss! If it doesn't happen on the first date, it's not a big deal. It's more important that you establish comfort with each other first.

"Personally, I don't always kiss on the first date!
I think a date still can be amazing if it doesn't end
with us kissing. As long as I feel comfortable around
him, enjoy his company, and find him attractive,
I don't mind waiting to kiss!"

—*Natasha, 31*

Make Her Laugh

Marilyn Monroe was onto something when she famously said, "If you
can make a woman laugh, you can make her do anything."

Humor is key in building attraction. It helps us get out of our
heads and into our bodies, which is required to forge a connection
with another person. This doesn't mean that you have to rattle off
one-liners or rehearse jokes ahead of time (nothing's less funny than
trying, and failing, to be funny). Just be present and look for opportunities to invite levity into your conversations. Details will inevitably
surface for you to playfully tease her about or challenge her on. It
goes without saying that these attempts shouldn't be offensive in
nature or highly personal—especially on the first few dates. You
have to know each other well enough for her to understand that
your comments are coming from a place of appreciation for her
flaws and quirks, not from a place of meanness. And don't dish it
out if you can't take it: there's a difference between self-respect
and self-regard.

Finally, it's just as important to find ways to laugh *together* as it is
to make her laugh. Look for common ground when it comes to things
you both find funny, like old movies, memes, current events, and the
like. This will help set the tone for your dynamic.

"Humor is a must for me. You don't have to be a stand-up comedian. Just be comfortable being weird with me and laughing will come naturally."

—Angela, 36

Flip the Script: Negging

"Negging," a term popularized by pickup artists, essentially means "light teasing." As I've indicated previously, this can be an effective form of flirtation, so long as it's not rooted in manipulation. The express purpose of "negging" should not be to make her desire you; any light teasing that transpires between the two of you should be rooted in your unique dynamic, with the goal being to engender intimacy. For example, if your date admits to hating a certain well-liked food, gently chiding her about it can be an indicator that (a) you've listened, and (b) you are close enough to each other to know and appreciate such small details.

Where men go wrong is when they overdo it. Teasing for the sake of teasing is a big turn-off. Although it may attract a woman who requires male validation, even at the cost of being disrespected, repeatedly and deliberately bringing down a woman's confidence via criticism will not endear you to her. Typically, a confident woman expects to feel better about herself in the company of a man who's pursuing her, not worse. As such, you need to consider whether the thing you're joshing your date about has the capacity to bring her more joy than it does hurt.

In general, it's a good idea to stay away from comments about her looks, friends, or family—at least while you're still getting to know each other. And in no context is teasing a woman about more personal matters, such as body odor or her tone of voice, acceptable.

Try Something New

When you're dating someone, you're writing a story together. Why not write a story you'd actually be interested in reading? The idea is to stand out quickly to your date by doing this differently. Not only will this position you as a unique guy, but it'll heighten the sexual chemistry when she sees your sense of adventure. To set this up properly, ask her how adventurous she is on a scale of 1 to 10. Then use the number she chooses as the meeting time for your adventure. From there, plan something simple that includes a break from the ordinary. Maybe it's stargazing. Maybe it's a rooftop dinner. Maybe it's a boat tour around the city. Find something to break her away from the day-to-day and fully zone in on you.

Build Rapport over Text

Whether we like it or not, we live in the era of text messaging. Gone are the days of long love letters. But that doesn't mean we can't use this convenient form of communication to add flavor to our dating life. I love short and witty text messages, because they're easy to digest and leave more to look forward to in person. Emojis are useful here, as are inside jokes and nicknames.

Whatever the basis of the texts, the point is to show her that she's more important than just any friend. She's someone you think about often! Simple texts such as "thinking about you" or "this reminded me of you" are a great way to increase intimacy and deepen your bond in between those first few dates. You can also use texts to compliment a woman and make her feel special.

REAL TALK

"I absolutely love it when I have banter with a guy over text. It's telling about his character, and, most importantly, it keeps things fun!"

—*Amy, 42*

DEEPENING THE CONVERSATION

If flirtation is a fine merlot, knowing when and how to take surface-level conversation to the next level is the steak. Either tastes great without the other, but they really sing when they're served together. Like flirting, deepening the conversation is a skill many men (and women!) struggle with. Whereas flirting requires you to make your attraction toward someone else plain, opening up to discuss deeper and more revealing topics requires vulnerability of a different kind—putting your feelings on the line without a guarantee of how they'll be received. I recommend using a process called "progressive disclosure," wherein you take your time revealing vulnerable truths about your past. Vulnerability requires openness, and the openness will develop over time. So don't be in a rush to share the things about you that are overly personal. Instead, focus on getting to know her story.

The best strategy I recommend to my clients when looking to deepen their surface-level date conversations is to use open-ended questions. They show your date that you really care and are curious to learn more about her story, which in turn will make her want to share more.

This may sound straightforward, but in order to ask good questions, you have to be an active listener. Active listening requires you to *really* hear what the other person is saying, rather than simply waiting your turn to speak. To convey understanding, you might offer words or gestures of affirmation, mirror their body language, or even paraphrase what they're saying. Pay attention to nonverbal cues: if one question causes her to hesitate or look away, you might want to redirect the conversation to a safer topic. In a sense, you want to lead the way, while checking in to make sure she's right there with you. A successful conversation allows you to learn your date's future vision for herself, her morals, and her values—without making her feel like she's at a job interview.

During the first few dates, there are some topics I recommend avoiding, such as the details of your past relationships, self-deprecation even when it's meant to be funny, politics, bodily functions or dysfunctions (for example: infections, your bowels, etc.), religion, and any other sensitive topics that may cause your date discomfort. Oversharing is just as harmful as undersharing. In fact, I usually tell my clients: when in doubt, leave it out . . . at least in the beginning! Once you've solidified your connection, you can flip that to "when in doubt, talk it out." But in the beginning, it's all about building up to that strategically.

Here are some open-ended questions you might consider when taking the conversation to the next level. (Keep in mind that, depending on your relationship, they might not all be appropriate for the first date.)

- Who are you closest to in your family?

- What are your best friends like?

- What does your life look like three years from today?

- What are your biggest dreams and ambitions? If you could be doing anything you like right now, what would that be?

- If you could live anywhere you want in the world, where would it be?

- What's something you learned from a past relationship?

- What are three things you have to do every day to feel like yourself?

- What's your experience dating in [location you live in] been like?

Part of taking the conversation—and relationship—to the next level involves talking about one crucial topic: your connection. Don't be afraid to ask someone you're seeing how she feels about you. It's okay to check in with her during or near the end of the date to get a sense of whether she sees this going anywhere. That said, until you've defined your relationship, you want to be wary of asking her if she's seeing other people, as that might make you look intrusive or overly controlling.

FINISH STRONG

So . . . you've just returned from your first date and are feeling all sorts of emotions. Perhaps some excitement, tinged with relief. A helping of hope, a hint of regret. Probably some mental exhaustion. And inevitably, you're asking yourself the ever-important question: *Do I want to see her again?*

To answer this question, get real with yourself: Are you attracted to her? Did she seem into you? Did you have fun? Does it seem like she wants what you want right now? Overall, if you never saw her again, would you be upset or indifferent? Consider whether other factors are holding sway over your feelings about her: Do you simply want to see her again because you're lonely? Sad? Unfulfilled? Horny? These factors are good motivations to get out there and date, for sure, but on their own, they are not great reasons to keep seeing one woman in particular.

We'll go over how to tactfully proceed once you've determined whether to pursue another date. In modern dating culture, many people avoid confrontation, because confrontation is hard. But you're not here to do things the easy way. You're here to do things effectively, which requires having the courage to be honest with yourself—and the people you date.

If You'd Like to See Her Again . . .

Many of my male clients struggle with securing second and third dates with the women they really connected with, because society has put the pressure on men to lead most of the early interactions. This isn't inherently wrong, but it can be quite intimidating.

To avoid what may feel like an unending deliberation over what kind of text to send (and when), it's ideal to secure the next date while you're on the first one. Of course, the presumption here is that your interest is reciprocated. Is she giving off signs she's attracted to you? Is conversation flowing smoothly? Has she given any indication of how she feels about you or the date? Has she mentioned, even casually, things you might do together in the future? If so, the best way to bring up the next date is to brainstorm ideas with her or reference something you've already discussed (e.g., a new restaurant you both want to try or a new movie you're both looking forward to seeing). This is why listening is so important!

If you decide to wait on scheduling the second date and to follow up instead, here's what I recommend: Assuming you're the one who asked for the date and took her out, hold off on contacting her afterward. The courteous move on her part is to thank you for the date. I'm not suggesting you invent a power struggle where one doesn't exist, but it's important that you gauge her level of interest before increasing yours. So await her feedback on the date. If she's interested, you should expect a text within the next two days thanking you for the date, or something along those lines. Should you prefer more certainty, I still suggest waiting at least 24 to 48 hours before reaching out. This gives her time to reflect on how she felt about the experience. Based on the enthusiasm in her response, you'll have more insight into how she feels about you.

If you do decide to reach out before she does, simply mention something that reminded you of the date and start a conversation that way. If she wants to see you again, she'll lead you in that direction. If she responds nicely but doesn't seem excited to meet again—for example, if her responses are curt or don't leave an opening for you to respond—then that's your cue that she's not interested. Do not push after that point. If a woman wants to see you again, she'll let you know! And if you're still not convinced, you can always verify it for yourself before moving on, asking her point-blank how she felt the date went and whether she'd be interested in a second. But be prepared for the truth, because it might sting.

MAKE YOUR MOVE

One quick idea for a second or third date: Ask her what she would eat for dinner if it were her last day to live. Then see if you can secure one of those foods for your next date!

If You Wouldn't Like to See Her Again . . .

It's never easy to let someone down. If she likes you, she will be upset. There's no avoiding that. But her feelings in the short term shouldn't stop you from making the courageous move and being honest and upfront with her. The longer you put off rejecting her, the more awkward and disappointing (for her) it will be down the road. Ultimately, it comes down to simply being a considerate human: being honest, though it may hurt, is a show of respect.

When you're letting her down, it's important to keep in mind that you don't need to share every little detail behind your decision. If, for example, her voice really got under your skin, she doesn't need to know that. She can't change her voice, and another guy might love that about her. Instead, give her only as much information as she needs to move on with grace. I always recommend that clients send a simple text thanking their date for coming out and letting them know that the romantic energy just wasn't there for them.

Be prepared to get back an unpleasant response or no response, period. But be reassured that she's just hurt, and that you did the right thing. Ghosting, or disappearing without a trace after a date (or—*gasp*—from a relationship), is a big problem in modern dating culture, particularly given how many people meet online. I know it can be extremely difficult to confront someone with the truth, but the truth brings closure, and you owe them at least that much.

REAL TALK

"If you're not feeling it, let me know. I'd rather be sad and get over something than be confused and holding on."

—*Heather, 22*

Go Forth and Prosper

Takeaways

- On a first date, you have the opportunity to dive into the world of another human, and that's sacred. Regardless of what happens on or after the first date, remember that. Gratitude is the best attitude to have in your dating life. When you're grateful, you exude the positive energy women are drawn to.
- Be sure to actively listen on your dates, and ask plenty of questions! The one asking the questions is the one in charge of the conversation.
- You should always gauge her level of interest before increasing yours. People value what they have to earn, and a woman should earn your attention.

Action Items

- Pick a movie (or even a reality show, if that's your thing) with a love story between two main characters. Observe the body language of the characters on the date. How do they indicate attraction to each other? How does the man use the woman's cues to escalate the intimacy in their interaction?
- Pick out a few of your best outfits—the ones you feel most confident in. Then schedule some time with a friend to snap 10 to 15 pictures of you doing different activities that highlight your personality. Send these pictures to a trusted friend (a woman's eye might help) and have them help you narrow them down for your dating profile.

Physical Intimacy and Sex

The birds and bees do it like it's no thing. Men follow their lead. But women need the light dimmed just right and the laundry done first. Is this way of thinking stereo-typical? Or is it true?

In this chapter, I'll share some insights with you on physical intimacy from a female perspective. We'll talk about what signs to look for before escalating touch, what turns a woman on (and off), consent, and more. Of course, some of what we'll cover in this chapter is probably review. But I'd still encourage you to tune in, because as society continues to evolve, so do the norms and expectations around sex.

THE IMPORTANCE OF
PHYSICAL TOUCH

Physical touch is key to deepening a connection with a woman—past "just friends." It communicates what words cannot, inviting sensuality and activating sexual energy between you and your date. That said, there's no need to rush this process. If touch is unwanted and you do it anyway, you run the risk of derailing an otherwise fruitful interaction.

When I talk about physical touch in this context, I'm obviously not referring to a handshake or high-five or a friendly pat on the back. I'm talking about touch that is expressly meant to induce sexual arousal—to convey an interest in something beyond friendship. Now, just because a touch is intended to induce sexual arousal doesn't mean it has to be sexual in nature—or that it has to lead to sex. Under the right circumstances, even the slightest physical touches can communicate this message, such as grazing a woman's hand or knee. Under the wrong circumstances, however, those same physical touches can feel like a violation. That's why it's critical not only to take heed of the advice in the previous chapter, but to be on the lookout for the right signals.

Look For the Signs

Our bodies reveal a lot about how we feel. Your date will give off verbal and nonverbal cues, either purposely or subconsciously, about whether she's ready for physical touch. It's up to you to read them correctly. Here's a helpful primer on what to look for.

Ask yourself: *Is she . . .*

Caressing her glass? This is a gesture of seduction, which may or may not be done consciously. Either way, it's a good sign to look for when deciphering her level of interest!

Looking at your lips? This may be a cue she wants to kiss you.

Making prolonged eye contact? In the proper setting, this is typically an indication of sexual interest or flirting.

Seemingly accidentally brushing her arms or knees against yours? Women often do this when they want to be closer to you physically.

Not letting go during a hug? A prolonged hug at the end of a date is a clear sign that a woman wants more physical proximity—and perhaps to be kissed.

Linking arms with you? This is a safe way for her to initiate touch with you, and a sign of permission for you to reciprocate that touch.

Resting her head on your shoulder? This is a sign of trust and security. A woman will do this when she feels comfortable in your presence.

Touching your arm or leg when she's laughing? This is an escalation cue that many women use to give men permission to touch them.

> **REAL TALK**
>
> "I will typically let a guy know I'm wanting him to be touchy with me if I start leaning up against him if he tells a joke or I'll intentionally brush his hand while sitting next to each other. I also will be super physical during laughing moments or happy moments. I won't make the first move, but I definitely leave the ball in his court."
>
> —*Eloise, 24*

Reorienting herself in a space to be closer to you? This is a less direct but still intentional move to indicate physical attraction.

Playing with her hair? Flipping, twirling, what have you—playing with one's hair is often flirtatious!

> ### REAL TALK
>
> "For me to let a guy know I'm open to physical touch would be to break the personal bubble. I feel like body language is the most important thing, so I would make a mental effort to hold longer eye contact and flip my hair and cross my legs in his direction."
>
> —Jane, 31

Slowing down or speeding up her speech? The former is a sign of seduction, the latter of nervous energy. Both can indicate interest.

Initiating a dance or any other activity that involves touch? This is a more direct sign of interest. If your date is intently initiating activities that involve touch, it's clear she's attracted to you!

> ### REAL TALK
>
> "I usually express that I'm open to [physical touch] if I also initiate [it]. Sometimes I've complimented their watch and kind of grabbed their hand to take a closer look at it (giving me an excuse lol) or compliment their shirt or something and then slightly touch or feel the fabric!"
>
> —Isabella, 24

By contrast, here's a helpful primer on signs she's *not* ready for physical touch.

Ask yourself: *Is she . . .*

Closing herself off to you? For example, is she folding her arms across her chest or leaning back in her chair?

Constantly distracted by her phone or other stimuli? Sometimes this is just a bad habit, but often, it's a sign she's just not that into you.

Intentionally creating barriers between you two? A good indicator of this might be if she keeps a purse on her lap.

Giving you a brief hug? Some people are just uncomfortable with physical touch. But if a brief hug isn't accompanied by any other sure indicators of interest, such as flirting or wanting to hang out more often, it's not a great sign.

Failing to initiate or maintain eye contact? Most people find eye contact uncomfortable, so if that's the case with your date, it could simply be that she's shy. But if it continues to be the case, it could be that she doesn't want to lead you on or invite you to escalate things physically.

Laughing obnoxiously or otherwise exhibiting excessive behavior? These kinds of behaviors suggest a lack of seduction. In other words, she's trying to do the opposite of making things romantic between you, sending an abundantly clear message that you're "just friends."

Pushing for the date or interaction to end earlier rather than later? Perhaps a more obvious sign: if your date wants out early, then it's safe to assume she's not interested.

Testing the Waters

Once you're aware of the signs, the following are all appropriate (and sexy!) ways to initiate physical touch:

Start with eye gazing. Find opportunities throughout your interactions to maintain eye contact, perhaps when you toast over drinks or during a moment of silence between conversation topics (let it linger). Prolonged eye contact is a great segue to physical touch. But note that you still need to make sure your date is on the same page as you.

Touch her shoulder. A great way to test your date's response to your touch is to start small. When you excuse yourself to go to the bathroom or get another drink, simply touch her shoulder and let her know you'll be right back. Observe her reaction: did she smile, or did she shrink from your touch?

REAL TALK

"I like when guys initiate physical touch when flirting with me! Even a quick shoulder nudge when cracking a joke, or gently placing his hand on my back if the moment is right. I definitely notice those small things."

—Isabella, 24

Lean in to her when you're talking. You need to close some of the space between you and your date to make touching feel more natural. As the conversation progresses, gradually lean in closer when you're talking. See how she responds. If she leans closer in turn, you might lean in even closer; if not, you might back up.

Place your hand on her back. When you're walking with your date, or waiting in line, try placing your hand on her back and see how she responds. A pro tip: Placing your hand too high on her back (near her shoulder blades) can read as platonic, but place it too low (near her butt) and you can come off as a creep. Placing it somewhere in the middle conveys the right kind of interest.

> **REAL TALK**
>
> **"I think it is completely natural for a guy on the first date to initiate physical contact such as a touch on the back. Honestly, if a guy went the entire first date without touching me in some way, I probably wouldn't go on a second date."**
>
> —*Maddi, 24*

Place your hand on her thigh. This move is more of an escalation than the others, so be sure to do it only after she's initiated physical contact with you via other means (perhaps by touching your hand or grazing your knee with hers). If you have that go-ahead, placing your hand on her thigh can be incredibly arousing and is a great way to set a romantic tone. But if she's not comfortable with it, then you definitely need to remove it (and perhaps apologize for moving too fast). I would also encourage you not to go any further than her thigh in the beginning!

"I am a big fan of 'courteous contact' on first dates, like hand on back, arm on the back of the chair I'm sitting on, hand on knee if asking me a question or if I want another drink . . . But just the knee! A kiss at the end is fine, but honestly, pushing any further than everything I mentioned is a turn-off."

—*Maria, 29*

Caress her face. Like the previous touch, this one is more of an escalation. You want to make sure you've received the right signs, have spent enough time together, and are in a private or intimate setting. To execute this, when you're sitting close together, lightly touch her cheek during the conversation. Maybe throw in a compliment for good measure. This touch should be more romantic than platonic, but also not *too* sexual, so don't leave your hand there too long. The idea is to use it as a segue to a kiss!

Tell her what you're thinking. Don't just wait for an opportunity to kiss her, create it! Some consider it cheesy or lame to ask a woman if you can kiss them. A much more assertive way to go about it would be prefacing that question with a statement of your desire: "I'm feeling a strong desire to kiss you right now, what are you feeling?" or "I'm thinking about how I want to kiss you right now. What are you thinking about?" This conveys both confidence (in your willingness to share how you feel) and respect (in your willingness to seek permission).

Put In the Work: Missed Signals

Whether it ends in a breakup or the refusal of a second date, we've all misread romantic situations before. In these cases, you feel not only the sting of rejection but the disorienting jolt of surprise: how many other signals have you misread?

Perhaps you failed to make a move, only to realize the signs were there all along. Or maybe you made a move and got rebuffed. Later in this chapter, you'll learn how to move at a rhythm with your date so that you feel more confident on this topic. To help you learn from your past mistakes, I invite you to reflect on the following questions.

1. Do you remember receiving one of the subtle cues mentioned in the Look For the Signs section (page 80) and not acting on it? What was your date's reaction? How did the date end?

2. Can you recall a time when your first date went great but you weren't able to score a second one? Looking back, what went wrong?

3. Can you recall a time when you were rejected for making a move (e.g., going in for a kiss)? Knowing what you do now, what could you have done better in that situation?

4. How have you gone about initiating touch before reading this chapter? Are there ways in which you initiate touch without thinking? If so, how are these touches received?

5. Of the tips mentioned in the Testing the Waters section (page 84), which fall most firmly in your comfort zone? Which ones fall outside of it, and why? Consider using the former, while working up to the latter.

6. What steps might you take to ensure you're not misreading or missing a woman's signals?

TURNING UP THE HEAT

It's one thing to escalate physical touch on a date, leading to that ever-important first kiss. As we all know, it's another thing entirely to make the transition from the first kiss to the bedroom.

Depending on your date's values, sex may not be on the table for quite some time (or until after marriage). Ideally, you want to tease out these details long before you make a move—sometime on the first or second date. Not only can this help you save face, it can help you save time: based on your expectations, your date's attitudes toward sex may be a deal breaker for you.

I realize there are unwritten rules that tend to govern heterosexual politics. Many men feel cultural or peer pressure to push for sex as soon as possible, whereas many women are pressured to coyly deflect or abstain. Though these pressures reflect outdated cultural mores, which designated men as the conquerors and women as passive objects of unvarnished purity, they are still sneakily pervasive in today's dating scene. (Consider, for example, the waiting game many women play when texting a guy back or the tacit impetus on men to make the first move.)

Personally, I was taught that I should refrain from sex until marriage, while the men around me were not—they were always after sex with whomever they could get. At face value, it might seem like men have it easier than women, but this idea comes with its own downfalls. For one, popular culture preaches to men that "more is better," and that the more women you sleep with, the more manly you are. But this path, while potentially exhilarating, often results in emptiness and confusion as to how to truly connect with women.

Freeing yourself from external pressures around sex is key to being your most authentic self—and forging a real, intimate relationship with someone. When you're ready to take things there, consider the following guidelines.

Follow Her Lead

As discussed earlier in this chapter, following your date's lead is the most organic and effective approach to initiating physical touch. It also ensures you obtain consent to escalate and shows you're a man who isn't desperate for things to progress faster than their natural pace.

Part of following your date's lead means moving deliberately. When you're kissing, for example, you don't just want to shove your tongue in her mouth and hope for the best. Take time to familiarize yourself with her lips and the circumference of her mouth. Kissing should be a tantalizing experience for both of you, not a fast pass to sex. Pause between kisses to play with her hair or to hold her tight. If you're standing, you might turn her around and put your arms around her waist, then kiss her neck slowly and make your way upward until you're behind her ears. The goal is to tease her playfully until she's dying to take your clothes off. Then, and only then, should you make moves toward the bedroom.

Activate Her Sexual Mind

You may have heard a variation on the adage: "Men make love with their bodies, but women make love with their minds." Of course, that doesn't mean women don't love how sex makes their body feel. But oftentimes, a woman's bodily desire is only awoken after the experience has already begun, whereas for men, bodily hunger is present before anything happens. To properly stimulate a woman, therefore, I would encourage you to first activate her sexual mind.

One way to do this is to set the stage properly. Women are sensual creatures, so focus on how you can activate all of your date's senses. For example, you can activate her sense of smell by diffusing some essential oils. You can activate her sense of touch by laying out fresh, soft sheets, perhaps even silk. You can activate her sense of taste by offering her some good red wine or dessert. You can activate her sense of sight by dimming the lights (and decluttering your bedroom ahead of time). You can activate her sense of sound by playing some low-key music you think would set the mood, depending on your preferences. By stimulating her senses in this manner, you're activating her sexual mind and inviting her to unleash her sexual prowess.

> **REAL TALK**
>
> **"The environment is so important. When a man puts intention into creating an ambiance that's sensually inviting, it's such a turn-on."**
>
> —*Shelly, 31*

Tease Her

Once you've activated her sexual mind, it's time to awaken her body. In movies, sex scenes are often sped up for the sake of entertainment, with quick cuts from passionate kissing to undressing to falling into bed and rolling around. Before you know it, the actors are catching their breath alongside each other, with a strategically placed sheet preventing any gratuitous nudity.

In the real world, of course, there's no reason to squeeze everything into a two-minute scene. To activate a woman's body, you need to focus on building tension. The way to do this, before the actual act of sex, is to tease her: touch her in ways that make her anticipate your next move, then pull back as soon as she thinks she knows what you're about to do. This builds up expectations only to tear them down. It drives women (and men) crazy—in a good way. Moreover, the uncertainty of it all will keep her entirely engaged and excited for sex, making the eventual act a fuller experience for both of you.

"I find orgasms akin to fine dining. The experience leading up to the first bite is the best part. If we don't rush dessert, why should we rush sex? There are so many delicious appetizers to be enjoyed before the main course."

—Amber, 29

Flip the Script: Consent *Is* Sexy

"Sex is like boxing," the comedian John Oliver once summed it up. "If both people didn't fully agree to participate, one of them is committing a crime."

Unfortunately, due to the pervasive cultural attitudes surrounding sex and masculinity, not all men concur on what "fully agree" really means. Although we continue to make progress as a society, we have been routinely conditioned to perceive women as incapable of making their own judgments. From a young age, women are often told, directly or implicitly, to be submissive when it comes to their bodies. To dress to entice the male gaze, before we even understand what that means. To prioritize a man's pleasure over our own. Thus, in the eyes of some men, a woman's "no" is actually a "maybe," or even a "yes." In some cases, a man may feel it is his role in this sexual dynamic to bend a woman's coy or evasive "no" into a "yes"—as if he alone knows what she "really wants."

The good news is that times are changing. The #MeToo movement, in particular, has shed a light on the frequent and pervasive instances of sexual harassment and assault (for some perspective, according to the Rape, Abuse & Incest National Network [RAINN], one out of six American women has been a victim of attempted or completed rape, and instances of sexual assault remain vastly underreported). Whereas some men will never change, most are eager to learn about and seek "enthusiastic consent"—by which I mean not simply the absence of a "no," but a clear and sustained "yes," through either body language or verbal cues, which can be revoked at any time. (An intoxicated person, it's worth clarifying, cannot issue consent.)

The kind of men who don't respect a woman's wishes might chafe at this concept. Nothing, they might say, could be less sexy than drawing up a contract every time you have sex. But there's nothing sexy about exhausting a woman's "no" in pursuit of a "yes," which may only surface out of a sense of resignation. What *is* sexy is taking her resistance seriously, being patient, evaluating what types of things she is and isn't cool with, and moving at a comfortable pace, thereby granting her the security to express her sexuality far more radiantly than she would had she been manipulated or coerced. In this way, consent is not a contract, it's a dialogue—oftentimes, an incredibly erotic one. After all, what could be sexier than confirming that the person you're attracted to feels the same way?

Getting Enthusiastic Consent

Here are some tools you can use to gain said "enthusiastic consent":

1. **Talk beforehand about what you both like and don't like.** One of my favorite exercises that I assign clients is a "nice, naughty, and never" list. In the "nice" column, they list things that they like but aren't crazy about (for example, having their ears licked). In the "naughty" column, they list their fantasies and desires (for example, being choked). On their "never" list, they share things they don't ever want (for example, anal sex).

2. **Keep the dialogue going.** Even after you make this list, it's important to continually get consent at every new level. I know that may seem like a lot of talking, and it is, but what could be sexier than talking about sex? Some questions you can ask during a sexual interaction: "Do you like that? Should I keep going? Can I touch you there? How does that feel?" In this way, you get consent without having to disrupt the flow.

3. **Confirm that you're on the same page afterward.** Last but not least, after all is said and done, confirm with the other person that you're on the same page. You can do this by simply asking them: "How was that for you? Did I do anything you really liked/didn't like? What would you like me to do differently next time?" By checking in after sex, you'll empower your sexual partner to give you advice on what exactly they want, setting the precedent for them to do the same.

WHAT WOMEN (ACTUALLY) WANT IN BED

When it comes to sex, the men I work with typically fall into two categories. Men in the first category take the double standard to its extreme by allowing their primal instincts to make their judgments for them. They lead a life of promiscuity with women they have no desire to connect with on an emotional level. Men in the latter category abstain from sex altogether and turn to other mediums for stimulation, such as pornography. Their fear is that they haven't accrued enough experience to pursue sex with real women.

In both cases, men face impediments to quality sex once they're in bed with a woman, in large part because they fail to meaningfully take into account a real woman's needs. It's quite simple: If you're not connecting on an emotional level, you're likely not listening well enough to really satisfy a woman. And if you're so consumed with your own fears and inexperience, you don't have the bandwidth to focus on someone else.

Fortunately, most men fall somewhere between these two extremes. But based on the fact that you've purchased this book, you're looking for ways to improve! There may be some habits you need to unlearn and others you'll want to acquire. Of course, no two women are turned on in the exact same way or by the exact same people or things, and this book is not a sex manual (not that a book can replace lived experience, anyway). That said, in the next section, I'll cover some of the most common misconceptions about female pleasure, address the anxieties many men feel in the bedroom, and provide some insider info on what women actually want, particularly when you're still just getting to know each other.

Communication Is Key

Sexual relationships, like all relationships, are built on a foundation of strong communication. Over a casual dinner or bottle of wine, ask her what her fantasies are, or simply the kinds of things she's found pleasurable based on her experience. Not only is this conversation stimulating and sexy—foreplay in its own right—you might also get a fuller picture of someone's desires than you would've during sex. It can also help alleviate performance anxiety: if you both know what to expect going into sex, you can relax and explore instead of having the added pressure of finding out what to do in the moment.

"Communication" doesn't necessarily mean a long, drawn out conversation about sex. Simply asking questions along the lines of "How would you like me to touch you?" and "How did that feel for you?" can be enough. With these questions, it's all about the delivery: it can be hard for some women to open up about what they really like, since society has conditioned them to be "good little girls" who don't challenge the status quo. But go the extra mile—it's always worth it!

And remember: Just because a woman in your past liked one particular thing doesn't mean the woman you're currently dating will, too! Asking, and not assuming, ensures you're both on the same page at all times (see more on page 94).

REAL TALK

"My current boyfriend is the only person who's asked me what I like and dislike in sex. I'm 49, and this is the first time I've enjoyed sex this much. What I think makes our communication the most effective is that it's an ongoing dialogue. I can confidently say that I finally feel like my pleasure matters, and that has made all the difference."

—Lauren, 49

Life Doesn't Imitate Porn

This may seem obvious, but it's worth reiterating: real sex is not like the sex you may see on your laptop. Indeed, many men experience erectile dysfunction because they're not receiving as much stimulation as they're used to with porn; others experience performance anxiety simply because a majority of their experiences with sex have taken place in front of a screen.

Many men who grew up (or are growing up) with the Internet received their primary course in sex education from porn. Some tend to think they know what women like because the women in the videos they watch act like their minds are being blown. But the adult entertainment industry was created for men by men, and the sex it represents is by and large highly superficial and fetishized. The women who work in porn are being paid to look like they're having the time of their lives, but according to a comprehensive research analysis synthesized in *The Case of the Female Orgasm*, about 75 percent of all women never reach orgasm from intercourse alone—that is, without the extra help of sex toys, hands, or tongue. So if you think you can simply pound away until she orgasms, think again!

Most women I talk to complain that porn has helped perpetuate an alternate reality wherein women are supplicants who enthusiastically perform all manner of sex acts. Yet this fantasyland cannot, and should not, be re-created in real life. Women want men to be more attentive to their unique needs and desires; they don't want to pantomime what you've seen paid actresses enjoy. Ultimately, this will lead to better sex for both of you. If you're willing to attend to her specific needs, she'll be more open to exploring your fantasies as well. And if you're going to watch porn, make sure you do so with a grain of salt. Your real-life sexual interactions may not emulate the porn you've watched, and that's okay. Try not to impose your ideas of what sex "should" be on anyone, and instead flow in the moment with what feels right, and always remember to communicate to achieve best results.

Let Her Come to You

In order for sex to feel enjoyable for both people, it has to be equally desired on both ends. When one person is constantly badgering the other to have sex, it starts to feel like a barking dog that needs to be petted all the time. It also makes the person constantly asking for it seem desperate and doesn't allow space for the other person to miss being intimate with them.

I know it can be hard to resist initiating sex with someone you're really attracted to, but as time goes on, it can be a good way to generate the sense of mystery and longing required to keep the flame burning. There are ways to invite sex without directly initiating it. For example, you could offer her a sensual massage or back rub. By arousing her senses in this way, you turn her on without pressuring her to have sex (while building the tension that may eventually lead to sex). So remember to give your partner space and let her come to you. I guarantee she will be more turned on as a result—and will reveal sides of herself you've yet to see awakened.

REAL TALK

"In order to miss something, by definition you have to be without it. If a man is always first to initiate sex with his woman, how will she have the experience of missing that? Man can still ravish his woman romantically while allowing her to invite the experience."

—Nivea, 33

Take Your Time

Just because you're raring to go, that doesn't necessarily mean your date is, too. When things get hot and heavy, it can be easy to overlook the previews in anticipation of the feature presentation. But many women don't orgasm through penetration alone, so by skipping foreplay, you risk finishing too early and leaving her empty-handed (a phenomenon many women know all too well). In a sense, you're also communicating to her that you're not concerned with her pleasure.

As I mentioned previously, women are conditioned to hold back on verbalizing concerns in the bedroom. So use foreplay as an opportunity to learn her likes and dislikes, and which areas of her body are more sensitive than others. Go slow and be gentle, especially when you're touching her genitals. Vaginal tissue can respond negatively to aggressive stimulation—the kind often seen in porn—before it's been properly lubricated. That doesn't mean that she won't *want* to move fast or for you to be more aggressive sometimes. But let her come to you for that when she's ready.

Keep an Open Mind

The final piece of advice I'd like to leave you with here is on incorporating toys and other novelties into your sexual life. I've already shared that, statistically, many women don't orgasm from penetration alone. In addition, a study published in *The Journal of Sex Research* found that using a vibrator can lead to multiple orgasms in almost half of all female users. The researchers also found that a majority of orgasms triggered by vibrator stimulation were more intense than those that were not. While this piece of information can seem off-putting to some, I promise that a toy isn't competition! A man who is truly confident in himself—and genuinely interested in his partner's needs—would never see it that way. Instead, he sees it as an opportunity to introduce some excitement and novelty into the bedroom and further enhance the experience for his partner.

Be open to other out-of-the-ordinary experiences as well, such as having sex in different places, exchanging dirty texts, or role-playing. So long as you've engendered a sense of trust, wherein your partner feels safe revealing her desires to you (and vice versa), you'll find that sex, rather than becoming boring or routine, will become a continual process of wonder and discovery.

Go Forth and Prosper

Takeaways

- When in doubt about when to have the first kiss, you can simply state your intentions verbally! It's an easy and consensual transition to making the moment happen.
- Most media involving sex between men and women is hardly depictive of the details that are necessary to create a satisfying experience for women. As a result, most women live out their sexual fantasies in their minds, where they can fully control the ways in which their desires are satisfied. (Hence the reason so many women flock to erotic novels and why, in recent years, movies such as *Fifty Shades of Grey* have gained so much traction.)
- Keep the lines of communication open. It's integral to building trust and creating a healthy sex life.

Action Items

- The next time you're on a date, pay special attention to the subtle cues your date gives you to initiate touch with her. Do you notice any of the cues mentioned in this chapter? Ultimately, it's up to you to act on them.
- Create a "nice, naughty, and never" list to share with a current or future partner (see page 94). Be sure to get detailed and really tap into what you like and don't like. This should be fun!

PART 3

THE REAL WORK

Up until this point, we've talked primarily about how to meet and court a woman. But once you've begun dating, the real work begins. In this section, we'll discuss making the transition from that initial spark to a committed relationship, as well as how to respectfully navigate breakups and bounce back from heartache.

From "Just Dating" to "In a Relationship"

Knowing who to date is just as important as knowing when (and how) to usher your burgeoning connection into a full-on relationship. The "dating" period provides an opportunity to learn about the woman you're interested in. If you rush your commitment to her, you risk not learning enough about each other. But if you wait too long, you risk letting the spark fizzle out. In this chapter, I'll provide some advice on taking the leap, while spotlighting some common pitfalls to avoid along the way.

MAKING THE LEAP

In every dating scenario, there are a few key checkpoints: The first kiss. When to have sex. Meeting each other's friends and family. But no juncture is more critical than deciding whether to enter into a committed relationship—beyond which lies the point of no return (or, rather, the point of no return without heartbreak and disappointment).

You also need to clarify whether a relationship is something you're both out to find. This may feel like a given to you, but particularly in today's world of online dating, increasingly casual sex, and swipe-based apps, it's not always as obvious as it initially seems. Be aware of the various labels a relationship can wear. "Hooking up" is often used to describe a casual relationship in which sex is present without an emotional connection. People in this dynamic understand that this connection is usually fleeting. There's an implicit understanding that both people in this dynamic are free to see and pursue other people at any time. Being "exclusive" or "in a relationship," by contrast, implies that you're physically and emotionally intimate, and committed to each other. In this case, there's a tacit or explicit understanding that you're not allowed to pursue other people outside of the relationship.

Now, here's the confusing part: the term "dating" itself, or terms like it (such as "seeing each other"), can mean different things to different people. To some women, "dating" means you're still seeing (or okay to see) multiple people; to others, "dating" implies you're only seeing each other but not yet in a committed relationship.

Ultimately, getting clear about what you're looking for in the early going can prevent you from hurting each other. Confusion kills. Clarity compels. If you do this too early, you may come on too strong. On the other hand, if you don't discuss it, she might assume you're seeing other people, and you might miss out on your chance to make your relationship with her exclusive.

Every relationship is different, but generally I recommend broaching this conversation once you've passed at least three of the following milestones together:

1. You've met each other's friends.

2. You've met members of each other's immediate family.

3. You've stayed the night at each other's houses.

4. You've spent extended periods with each other (an entire weekend, for example).

5. You've spoken about the future and confirmed that your visions overlap.

6. You've taken a trip together (out of the city/state/country you're in).

7. You've borrowed or lent each other a valuable personal item, such as a car.

8. You've shared painful stories from your past.

9. You've allowed each other to be in your homes when you weren't there (say, while you were at work).

10. You've overcome a challenge together and/or been there for each other when you're down and out (disappointed, sick, etc.).

I always remind my clients that rejection and heartbreak don't destroy people; ambiguity does. It's the "what ifs" and the "if onlys" that linger in our minds when other memories fade, which make it harder for us to trust again. Hope can be anathema to dating: oftentimes, it's the reason people get stuck in mediocre and toxic relationships. So make sure you're on the same page. When you choose a partner, you choose a story. Choose wisely.

In the pages to follow, I've provided a few specific tips to keep in mind when making this all-important transition.

Don't Lead Her On

The last thing you want to do is to lead someone on and set them up for a fall. If you know you don't want to be in an exclusive relationship, for example, it's a good idea to communicate that from the get-go. Just because she doesn't ask you about this point-blank doesn't mean it's fair to spend an ample amount of time together before revealing this position.

Oftentimes, leading someone on is not a conscious decision. Well-intentioned people make this mistake all the time because they're unsure of how they feel and what they want. They might hold out hope of developing feelings where there are none, or *want* to want a committed relationship, even though their actions suggest otherwise. In these instances, it's important to take a step back and see the situation from her side: How is your uncertainty manifesting itself in the relationship? How might it end up hurting her? When in doubt, be upfront about your uncertainty. See if it's something you can resolve together. And if you're dating a woman who seems more into you than you are her, let her know. Confrontation is uncomfortable in the moment, but it will spare her feelings in the long run. You don't need to disclose every detail. I usually advise clients to say something along the lines of, "I'm not feeling the romantic energy/chemistry/passion between us, and I just want to be honest about that because I believe you deserve someone who feels the same way about you that you do about him."

> **REAL TALK**
>
> **"It really sucks when someone leads you on with zero intention as to why. I would much rather someone shock me with the truth upfront then drip the news over a slow burn."**
>
> —*Nina, 38*

Be Honest with Yourself

Committing to another person can feel like a responsibility when you're ready for it and a burden when you're not. Many men (and women) experience anxiety around commitment, either because it will limit their freedom to do as they please or, more likely, because they're afraid of going all in only to lose everything.

So be honest with yourself. Is your freedom to do what you want with whom you want more important than having the support of someone you can count on? Do you actually want to be single, or are you just afraid of getting hurt? Conversely, are you entering into a relationship because you think it's what you're supposed to do to be happy? Are you afraid of being alone? Do you just want to be validated by another person? These are important concerns, but they aren't the primary reasons to be with someone. Each decision has its pros and cons, and it's up to you to ensure that your decision reflects what you need at this point in your life. Be true to yourself, and honor where you're at in your journey.

Put In the Work: What's the Potential?

How do you tell whether a woman you're seeing is worth progressing into a relationship with?

One way I help clients answer this question is by having them categorize the value of the match as low, medium, or high.

Here's a quick quiz designed to help you make this categorization. Answer each question yes or no:

1. For the most part, do your values align?

2. Would you proudly introduce her to your parents?

3. Is she intelligent?

4. Does she share your passion for life?

5. Does she make you laugh?

6. Does she turn you on?

7. Does she have a growth mindset?

8. Does she make a good team player?

9. Does she get along with your tight-knit circle of friends?

10. Is she her own person?

11. Does she challenge you and help you grow?

12. Does she make you feel like a better man?

13. Are you looking for the same thing out of a relationship?

If you answered "yes" for most or all of these questions, congratulations! Why? Because you're not just putting yourself out there and hoping for the best. You've got a high-value match.

If you answered "no" for a majority of these questions, it may be time to get real with yourself. Why are you really pursuing this connection? If it's time to walk away from a low-value match, do yourself (and her) a favor by doing so. If you're somewhere in between, then continue to see her until you have a surer position. Things take time, and you don't want to write someone off too quickly.

Don't Assume Exclusivity

You should never assume exclusivity just because it *feels like* you're a couple. Have the talk! As my former supervisor used to say, "When you assume, it makes an ass out of you and me." When in doubt, talk it out. There's no black-and-white process when it comes to having the exclusivity talk. It just needs to happen. A natural way to ease into this conversation is to check in several weeks after beginning to date (if everything is progressing well) and just ask: "So how do you feel about our connection? Where do you see it going?" You may not even have to be the one to broach this conversation. She might beat you to it. Hearts are broken when exclusivity is assumed without a proper conversation. Just because a woman is fully present with you when you're together doesn't mean she's not seeing other men. Usually, even if she is seeing other people, deep down she knows who she really wants to be with. So don't be afraid to ask her when it feels like the right time.

Discuss Your Boundaries

Physical boundaries are, for the most part, easy to detect, because social norms orient us accordingly. You would not punch a random person in the supermarket line or throw water at the person sitting behind you at a restaurant. Emotional boundaries, however, are easier to trespass because feelings aren't as straightforward. So if you know yourself to be a giving person who's concerned with the well-being of those around you, make sure you're also respecting your own boundaries in your dating life. It's easy to justify another person's behavior because you like them and want to give them the benefit of the doubt. But as I always say to my college friend who's been on a decade-long streak of dating married men "in the process" of leaving their wives: If it walks like a duck and quacks like a duck, guess what? It's a duck!

Boundaries teach people to treat you the way you want to be treated. When behavior is negatively reinforced, we're less likely to repeat it. The opposite is also true. If your date is late three times in a row and you smile and say nothing, you've just given her permission to continue behaving in the same way.

Now that we've covered the importance of setting boundaries, let's discuss the process by which to do so. A boundary is made up of three parts: acknowledging how the problematic behavior makes you feel, suggesting the desired behavior moving forward, and explaining that there will be consequences if the problematic behavior is repeated. The most important thing to take away from this is that a boundary without clear consequences for violating it isn't actually a boundary. It's an opinion. So if you expect your boundary to stick, make sure to include all three parts in it.

Discover How You Navigate Conflict Together

Entering a relationship is a lot like buying a car. Not only do you have to know what you're looking for, but you have to be prepared for problems that come up once you drive the car off the lot. When we're in love, we tend to ignore what we don't like and focus intently on what we do. What results is a mirage that, if left unchecked, can lead us into a situation we haven't thought through. For this reason, I advise my clients to create "intentional tension" early on in courtship to assess how they deal with conflict as a couple. This means putting yourself in a situation with the other person where there is a problem that needs to be solved to test your chemistry as a team.

One example of this is going to an escape room for one of your dates. Escape rooms are great because they force you to solve a mystery together. Another good example is playing a sport or a game that puts you on the same team. You can learn a lot about your potential for success with someone by working through a problem with them. Do they think on their feet? Are they a solution-finder or a complainer? Do they give up easily, or are they persistent? Committing to another person is a big gamble, but this is one way to mitigate the risk.

"People put their best foot forward when they're attracted to someone. My experience is that the more realism I can experience with a man early on, the better."

—Eva, 30

DATING PITFALLS

Despite one's best efforts, we're all prone to certain unhealthy behaviors en route from "just dating" to "in a relationship." In the pages to follow, I'll identify some of the most common pitfalls men experience at this stage, as well as some concrete advice on how to avoid them.

You Become the "Jealous Boyfriend"

The Pitfall: It's not wrong to experience jealousy with someone you're dating. Jealousy is a natural response to wanting to protect the people we care about the most. But what starts out as a well-intentioned response can morph into a toxic habit if left unchecked. When you start trying to control your partner's behavior—for example, where she hangs out or who she sees—your harmless jealousy has spun out of control. If this continues, you'll push your partner away and spoil your chances of enjoying a healthy relationship.

How to Avoid It: Learn how to recognize your jealousy when it's triggered. Ask yourself: Am I jealous because my partner is crossing an obvious boundary? Or am I jealous because I'm feeling insecure in our relationship?

If your partner *has* crossed a boundary, you want to make that clear, while separating her behavior from your feelings. A good way to frame this is: "When you did [upsetting behavior], it made me feel like [reaction you had]. I know you probably didn't intend it that way, but that's how it came off to me. In the future, could you be mindful of doing [upsetting behavior] and instead try [desired new behavior]? If that's too much to ask, maybe we should have an honest conversation about our boundaries and what we expect of each other. What do you think?"

If you're feeling insecure because of something she has no control over—for example, someone trying to hit on her—ask yourself: What is the root cause of my frustration? Is there a way to transmute my jealousy into inspiration? We often feel jealous of people because we want something they have. How can you develop the aspects of yourself your jealousy has triggered?

You Expect Too Much

The Pitfall: No matter what you've been told, when it comes to romance, it *is* possible to have too much of a good thing. In other words, you don't want to rely on a romantic partner to fulfill *all* your needs. Personally, I used to believe my romantic partner had to be everything at once: a lover, best friend, and confidant. I placed all this pressure on one person, and inevitably this pressure exploded in my face. The bottom line is, one person can't be everything for you. They can't be your confidant, best friend, business mentor, *and* mysterious lover. While movies may make it seem like such a person exists, reality proves them wrong time and again.

How to Avoid It: Learn how to maintain your own happiness and fulfillment. Don't wait for your partner to add flavor to your life, because if you do, you're at their mercy. Make your life so exciting that it becomes an enticing invitation. Don't neglect your friendships when you start seeing someone. Keep up with your loved ones. Continue to seek satisfaction from your career and/or other interests.

Remember to diversify the ways you meet your needs so that you're never leaning too heavily on one person. Oftentimes, when people are discussing their ideal partner, you'll hear them say, "I'm looking for my best friend." But your romantic partner doesn't need to replace your best friend. They have their own role to play in your life, and you (and your partner) ought to appreciate it.

Flip the Script: The "Friend Zone"

With the exception of the dentist and the line at the DMV, few places are spoken about with as much dread as the "friend zone." Simply put, the friend zone is what happens when one person wants a romantic relationship, while the other person just wants to be friends. Oftentimes, being "friend-zoned" refers to the person on the receiving end of the romantic interest deciding to keep the relationship platonic. According to popular lore: Once you're in the friend zone, there's no getting out. It's purgatory!

Is this true? Well, kind of. The friend zone *can* exist in real life. Certainly, there are women out there who get off on knowing guys are into them, even though they have no intention of dating them. There are also those who will insist on using you as a kind of human teddy bear. She'll lean on you when she needs you, then ditch you as soon as she's recharged. This is draining. And if you're not careful, it can keep you from seeking out other women to date.

Of course, instances of being friend-zoned are far less common than movies and TV shows would have you believe. It's unfair to assume that every girl you harbor feelings for is consciously putting you in the friend zone. More likely than not, they're unaware of your interest and genuinely want to be your friend. Alternatively, they might be in a spot in their lives where they can't make room for you as anything more. Perhaps she's already dating someone else, or simply not dating at all.

It's also not true that the friend zone is inescapable. Some of the best relationships start out as friendships! The difference is, someone in those friendships had the confidence to make a move. When you consider a relationship in terms of the "friend zone," you're inherently taking a passive stance—the platonic nature of your dynamic is something happening to you, rather than something you have the power to change. You're waiting to be promoted to boyfriend without taking the kind of bold action required to earn it.

You Move Too Quickly

The Pitfall: You're really into the girl you're dating. Everything is moving smoothly. In fact, things are going so well that you start shifting your entire life around to make more room for this relationship.

The problem is, you don't really know whether she's ready to accept this role in your life or whether she's even right for it. When we first start dating someone, it's natural to be on our best behavior and, simultaneously, to extend the benefit of the doubt to the other person. While there's nothing inherently wrong with wanting things to work out between you, rushing into a commitment can create significant blind spots, which may not reveal themselves until it's too late.

How to Avoid It: Slow down. Take your time to really know the person you're dating, in a number of environments and circumstances. Try not to channel all your energy into one person too quickly. Things take time to develop, and you should be using this period to clarify what you want.

To help you decide whether you're really ready for something more, I recommend sharing a few milestones first (see Making the Leap, page 106). Ask questions about her past relationships, temperament, family, values, and goals in life. Every relationship moves at its own pace; there doesn't need to be a specific timeline. Be mindful of getting ahead of yourself and assuming things about the other person instead of letting them show you who they really are. When you start making excuses and justifying another person's bad behavior, that's a telltale sign that things aren't right.

You're Plagued by Neediness

The Pitfall: When you meet someone you like, and who likes you back, there is a level of excitement that comes from inviting them to share their life with you. But it's easy for this excitement to mutate into an insatiable need for validation: if two are to become one, so to speak, it's only natural for you to seek constant approval from the person you're dating. But these expectations are impossible for anyone to meet, resulting in feelings of resentment and blame. Ultimately, nobody wants to be with someone who would feel useless without them. That's the role of a parent, not a partner.

How to Avoid It: The first step I take with all my clients is to help them heighten their sense of self-awareness. I have them sit down and take an inventory of their prior relationships and/or attempts at them: What patterns do they notice? What types of people do they usually go for? How do they feel about dating, and how has that impacted their behavior and results?

> Try using these questions to find the common denominator in your story. We must remind ourselves that we are solely responsible for making ourselves feel worthy. Everyone else in our life should only add to that worthiness, including our romantic partner. Set the right tone and boundaries from the beginning, both with yourself and with the person you're seeing: What will and won't you be accountable for? Make introspection a habit. Ask yourself: How am I showing up for myself lately? Is there any way I could do better? Am I leaning too heavily on my partner? Am I expecting too much of them or vice versa?

Keep the Mystery Alive

The Pitfall: In the words of the renowned marriage counselor Esther Perel: "Everyone should cultivate a secret garden." The paradox in romantic relationships is that intimacy requires closeness, but passion needs enigma. The two-step of creating closeness and maintaining space is delicate and nuanced; managing it more deliberately puts you, and your burgeoning relationship, in a position to succeed.

How to Avoid It: In order to maintain your "secret garden," you need to refrain from sharing every little thing with your partner. You want to leave some stuff up to their imagination. I advise my clients to "say one less unimportant thing every day." It may sound harsh, but this is a great rule for life, too. This one rule will make you more succinct and intentional. It will also increase the odds of your partner tuning in when you have something special to share.

Go Forth and Prosper

Takeaways

- Remember to be honest with yourself about what you want, and make sure your dating behavior reflects that—particularly en route to a committed relationship.
- One way to avoid the "friend zone," particularly when you're meeting someone new, is to avoid ambiguity altogether. If you're going out together, make it clear that it's a date, either beforehand or during. The longer you wait to define the relationship, the more likely she'll consider you "just a friend."
- Entering a new relationship can be very scary. Sometimes it looks like you're giving up your autonomy. But I want you to look at it differently. You're writing a story with a partner alongside you. While it's scary not to know what the future holds, it's also what keeps things interesting. So embrace the journey, and trust yourself to choose well.

Action Items

- Write down triggers that have made you feel jealous or compare yourself to other men in the past. What do you notice? What areas of yourself can you improve to start diminishing those feelings when they arise?
- Generate a list of "unimportant topics" you might hold off on sharing with a new partner and create your very own secret garden. The idea here is to start engaging the spirit of enigma and becoming more deliberate about what you share.

Breaking Up and Getting Back Out There

If you're going to play to win, you have to risk losing. Most people avoid the risk altogether by simply playing not to lose. They settle for mediocre careers and suboptimal relationships, the potential losses of which won't sting quite as badly. But if you want to be among the few who dare to live boldly, you must accept disappointment and heartbreak as features of the game, not bugs. In this chapter, we'll discuss healthy ways to break up, heal, and get back out there. My goal isn't to discount the pain of breakups. Rather, it's to make the process kinder on everyone involved, no matter what led to the unraveling of the bond.

BREAKUPS ARE HARD. FOR A REASON.

The road to love is littered with relationships that don't work out. But just because something isn't working out doesn't mean you owe any less respect to your partner.

All relationships require maintenance. They're a constant negotiation between two independent human beings who've chosen to intertwine their lives. Along the way, things can get messy. You might say things you don't mean, or never say the things you do. Once-clear and rigid boundaries can become fuzzy and flexible. You and your partner can do everything right, and the relationship can still end up being wrong. That's okay: the notion that a relationship is a failure because it doesn't last forever is false, not to mention useless. It's much more useful to measure a relationship's success by your ability to grow from it.

Even the most painful lessons in life are just that—lessons. They make us stronger and more resilient, helping us get clarity about what we want moving forward. Over time, you'll see that every relationship builds upon the one before it, resulting in the man you are today—the man who may be ready, finally, for the one relationship that lasts forever.

Among the biggest challenges of breaking up is knowing when it's time to do the deed. Sometimes, the signs are unmistakable. Other times, things are just good enough to not let go, or simply too hard to let go of. It's in these gray areas that relationships flounder, dragging on far longer than they should.

In these situations, I encourage my clients to trust their intuition. But if intuition speaks, the mind screams. The latter overpowers the former 9 times out of 10. That's unfortunate, given the veracity and foresight of our intuition. It's important to notice and interrogate small inklings of doubt, and to lend your intuition the headspace necessary to steer you in the right direction.

Once you've determined that a breakup is necessary, the next challenge is to proceed with care, caution, and respect. In the following sections, I'll lay out some advice to avoid an ugly breakup, no matter how the relationship unraveled.

The Hallmarks of a Bad Breakup

Whether you like it or not, breakups bring to the surface many suppressed or underlying feelings: fear, anxiety, guilt, disappointment. What builds and defines one's character, however, is how you respond to these feelings. Do you run away when things are hard, or do you stay the course? Do you assume the worst in people or give them the benefit of the doubt? Do you speak the truth even when it's hard, or do you skirt it to avoid confrontation?

Burning bridges may feel like the easiest route when you're in the moment, but over the long haul, it can create a lot more problems than it's worth. Our culture celebrates coming together but condemns the end of a relationship. It doesn't need to be that way. If you exit your relationship with the same amount of grace you walked into it with, you will undoubtedly set the stage for expedited success moving forward. Not only will you feel more wholesome in your dating endeavors, but when you look back, you'll have something to be happy about.

In the following sections, I'll highlight a few common hallmarks of a bad breakup.

REAL TALK

"What hurts the most is sharing so much with someone, from your half-chewed gum to your worst childhood secrets, then having them flip the script on you and treat you like a stranger."

—*Rania, 30*

YOU START SABOTAGING YOURSELF
AND THE RELATIONSHIP

Of all the realizations I experienced during my coaching training, one of the most interesting was this: the primary impediment to living out our dreams is none other than ourselves. Relationships are no different. Sometimes, a relationship may seem too be good to be true only because we refuse to believe we're worthy of the love we so desire (and deserve). Of course, this is less a relationship issue than a personal insecurity—a matter of thinking, deep down, that you're simply not good enough.

What usually follows is a vicious cycle of self-sabotage. Low self-esteem manifests itself as unchecked jealousy, betrayal, or otherwise repellent behavior, which succeeds in pushing away the person you love and reinforces the notion that you're not worthy of their love. The natural conclusion of this self-sabotage is a premature (or altogether avoidable) breakup.

There are several other reasons one would engage in these behaviors. Oftentimes, it's a way to avoid taking responsibility. Rather than being transparent about your dwindling feelings, you may instead choose to exhibit behaviors that you know will provoke the other person to end it. This often happens subconsciously because the fear of being truthful is too much to bear.

Be wary of self-sabotaging behaviors, and when you catch yourself in them, pause and ask yourself: Is there really something worth fighting over here? Or is this a pattern of behavior? What am I afraid of, and how is that fear manifesting itself in my actions? What in my past makes me distrustful and unable to fully let go and trust that I am wanted and loved?

I realize these questions can be hard to answer. But, as I tell my clients, "When you can name it, you can tame it." Your past doesn't have to determine your future.

TRANSITIONING TO FRIENDSHIP TOO SOON

Whether the relationship ends on a good note or a horrendous one, it can be hard to cut all ties. Just because you've decided intellectually that a relationship has run its course, your body doesn't necessarily agree. But trying to switch off the romance before you're really ready in an effort to save a friendship can exacerbate the situation. It can hold you back from moving on as quickly as you would if you severed ties, and let's face it: You're not friends. At least, not yet. Friendship with an ex is totally possible, but in due time, with due diligence. Once you've both reestablished your lives without each other, then and only then can you reestablish them with each other as friends.

GHOSTING

I had a female client ask me once, "How can I break up with my boyfriend without hurting him?" I didn't have to think long. "You can't," I replied.

Needless to say, she wasn't pleased to hear that. There's a reason heartbreak and breakups share the word "break." You're *breaking* a bond, and that's painful no matter what. Those with integrity understand this somber reality but take responsibility for their wish to go through with it anyway. People without a certain level of integrity may instead opt for what's easy: ghosting. When a breakup is mutual, there's less reason to let things implode. But when you're the one walking away, it can be tempting to not want to confront the reality of hurting the other person. Instead, it might be easier to just close camp and go about your business. This isn't necessarily malicious. It's simply an "easier" route to doing what's necessary, which is liberating the other person with the truth. I know it can seem cruel in the moment, but the kindest thing you can do is be honest about the fact that you're no longer interested.

Flip the Script: "It's Not You, It's Me"

Ah, the old adage "It's not you, it's me." No doubt, you've either heard or spoken a version of this sentiment at some point. But is there truth to it?

Definitely. The fact of the matter is, if someone's not a good fit for us, it's because we're not a good fit for them either, and as such, we are indeed the obstacle standing in the way of the relationship.

But are there more tactful (and less predictable) ways of delivering the same sentiment? Certainly. All too often, people are afraid of being honest because they don't want to offend anyone else. But humans are more resilient than we give them credit for. And chalking up the breakup to "It's not you, it's me" amounts to a kind of cop-out— a pat way of avoiding the messier truths. It's nice to offer up a cliché like this; it's kind to be more forthcoming. If it really is you, not her, why is that?

Are you not ready to date again because you're still in love with your ex? Are you simply not super attracted to this person? Do you feel more friendship vibes? Offering more of an explanation takes this cliché and flips it on its head in a way that's constructive and forward-moving.

The Hallmarks of a Good Breakup

We often hear the breakup horror stories: The tawdry affair. The nasty spats. The lawyers. The custody battles. Rarely, however, do we hear about two mature adults who consciously decided not to make each other's lives miserable because they no longer see romantic potential in each other.

Unlike a toxic breakup, a healthy breakup is rooted in respect for the other person, even when that seems like the least available possibility to you. There's no vengeance or malice. Rather, there's empathy. Depending on how things ended, empathy might not feel like a readily available option to you. In those cases, your values and integrity can serve as tools in your arsenal to navigate this. Choosing to be the bigger person and administer respect where it might seem undeserved will serve you far more in the long run than if you lean into your desire for vengeance.

In the pages to follow, I'll give you some pointers on how to conscientiously deal with a breakup—and how to use your breakup to power a breakthrough.

> **REAL TALK**
>
> **"I never understood why we make such a big fuss at the start of a relationship, but then when it ends the tendency is to leave through the back door and let it slam. I've made a point to exit my relationships with as much grace as I came into them with, and that has made all the difference."**
>
> —*Nia, 37*

YOU LEAD WITH YOUR HEART

I grew up listening to R&B songs that ruminate on unrequited love and watching rom-coms where the staples of breakups were pints of ice cream and booze. But numbing yourself with sugar and alcohol is hardly a recipe to heal from heartbreak. As I write this, I can still vividly recall my last breakup—one I did not see coming. Was it painful? You bet. But given all the experience I'd gained as a dating coach, I refused to let things end the way I'd been taught they needed to.

Against all odds, I was back on my feet several days after things ended, and my heart was fully healed a few weeks later. I firmly believe it was because we led with our hearts on our way out of the relationship. That is to say, we were kind to each other. We were honest and compassionate. We gave each other space to say everything that needed to be said. Even though I didn't see it coming,

I surrendered to it. A relationship can't survive with only one person fighting for its success. I figured, if I was already losing this person as a romantic partner, did I really need to lose him entirely as someone I once cared about? Or was there another way to negotiate with reality and salvage our connection even if it was no longer a romantic one?

NO CONTACT

I'll admit that when that last relationship ended, I was really hoping my ex and I could stay in touch. Surely, I thought, since we had ended on such a beautiful note, it could be possible. But rarely does this hope align with reality. Simply put, when you're still tethered to a person you're simultaneously trying to detach from, it delays your acceptance of the harsh reality: that you're no longer together. Your dynamic has shifted, and your actions must reflect it.

Thus, I highly encourage you to practice "no contact" after the decision to split up has been made: no calling, no texting, no liking each other's posts on social media. If your ex reaches out, the most responsible and useful way to handle it is to simply find out their intention, then kindly state your intention to not be in contact at the moment. This is true whether you're the dumper or the dumpee. If you ended it, then you need to respect your ex and give them space to heal. If you're the dumpee, you also need to resist the urge to seek your ex's support. I know it can be challenging to distance yourself from the person who would normally provide you comfort, but alas, that's how breakups work. You have to do what's necessary for you—and, ultimately, your ex—to move forward. Keep them out of sight until they're out of mind.

MAINTAIN YOUR INTEGRITY

In the beginning of your relationship, you both put your best foot forward, treating each other with kindness and respect. You wanted to make things work. When it all ends, though, it's easy for those attitudes to darken under the cloud of the breakup. All the energy you initially spent making the relationship great may come out the other side nasty and bitter.

Ultimately, having integrity is just as critical at the start of a relationship as it is at the end of one. If, for example, you wouldn't flirt with your girlfriend's best friend, you certainly shouldn't be doing it once she becomes your ex. But it requires a level of integrity to practice restraint when it counts—and it always counts. Burned bridges serve no one. Delaying momentary pleasures in the name of integrity is far more fulfilling than giving in to your primal instincts in the moment.

In the age of social media, in particular, a breakup isn't a private affair. It can be a tabloid of torture. So be kind and courteous with how you show up after things end. When you reenter the dating scene, don't broadcast that online right away. There's no need to be public about your personal life right after a breakup. Be gracious, even if that's not what you get in return.

DEALING WITH HEARTBREAK

Let's say you're on the receiving end of a breakup. How do you begin to recover? Unfortunately, much of the advice we typically receive to "help us" actually promotes escapism and victimhood, or villainizing and/or forcefully forgetting an ex. Even the word "breakup" itself denotes such a negative experience. Combine this with dating apps and social media and you have an insidiously toxic concoction with which to numb the pain. My take? Screw that. I founded my career on the belief that humans are resilient and capable. I believe that if we learn how to ally with our minds and bodies during this painful process, we can bring about faster and more effective healing.

In order to do so, however, you need to treat yourself with compassion and give yourself the space to heal. It's all too easy to fall down the rabbit hole of never-ending "what ifs." Forgive yourself for any mistakes you made and focus on self-love. Fill your fridge with healthy foods, your mind with good books, your calendar with supportive people. And take your time: I myself have been guilty of putting on my big girl pants before I was ready.

Healing won't be a linear process. Some days will be easier; others will feel unbearable. The tendency to jump from empathizing with your heartbreaker to despising them is completely normal. The most important thing is to focus on moving forward. Moving forward isn't the same as moving sideways—that is, distracting yourself from reality by filling up on beer or sleeping with random women. No judgment here, of course, but as distracted as you may be, if you truly expect to move on, you must give yourself an opportunity to process what happened. And remember: a breakup doesn't have to break you.

Put In the Work: How to Mend a Broken Heart

Create a list of things you love doing. Take a trip to somewhere beautiful and get offline for a few days. Volunteer for a good cause. Hang out with friends you were too busy to see when you were dating. Visit a new city. Do what you need to do to feel like you again, sans alcohol, sans random chick. Surround yourself with good people who care about you. Nourish your body with nutritious and delicious food. Listen to uplifting music. Get good sleep. Meditate. Journal your emotions about what happened. Include what you've learned from the relationship and what type of partner you want to attract moving forward.

GETTING BACK OUT THERE

Everyone is different. But a good indication that you're ready to date again is when time starts passing without you thinking about your ex. Once you start to feel present in your life again, that's when you know you're beginning to move on. There's no "ideal time" to put yourself back out there, so don't be in a rush. Once it's time, you'll feel it. Suddenly a heaviness will be lifted, and you'll feel excited about life again. That's when you know!

Grief has a unique way of making us feel the range of emotions we've somehow been able to avoid. Breakups are no exception. Often following a breakup, we feel loss, confusion, and perhaps even longing, yet simultaneously there's a feeling of oneness. This happens because our soul yearns for the full range of emotions. That's how we know we're alive, by feeling everything that belongs to this human experience. In that way, breakups can serve our mission to live fully.

The Wrong Turns

We've talked a lot about what to do after a breakup, but there's an equally long list of what not to do. In the following sections, I'll speak to some of the wrong turns people can make when getting back into the dating scene after a while.

GETTING UNDER SOMEONE TO GET OVER SOMEONE ELSE

I hinted at this in the last section—and perhaps you've heard the saying—but it's definitely worth diving into. As a means of getting over someone, pursuing and/or engaging in empty sex is futile. You might think of it as short-term gain, long-term pain. Sure, getting laid will get your mind off your ex temporarily, but in the long term it could harm more than it helps. Of course, there's a caveat here. Sometimes, a rebound might be what's necessary for you to finally move on. If you feel genuinely connected to someone new after your breakup, it could serve your healing process to explore that. So long as you're aware of your intentions, you can allow yourself to enjoy the experience. But in the long term, you may simply prolong an unavoidable process of healing.

So, as much as your friends might urge you to get back out there, don't go looking for a rebound when you ought to be directing your energy inward and focusing on your health, your mental wellness, your close social circle, and your happiness.

WRITING OFF ALL WOMEN

An all-too-common byproduct of a bad breakup is the tendency to take the pain caused by one person and transpose it onto an entire sex (think of women who proclaim they're "swearing off all men," or men who suggest "all women are crazy"). I know it's easy to feel this way after a breakup. But women don't want to be around a man who's jaded and bitter. And as much as you may think you can hide it under a wry smile or disguise it as sarcasm or irony, we can smell it from a mile away. Don't yield to the weight of your past baggage, then look to slough it off on someone else. Take the time to get over your breakup, so your feelings toward the next person you date aren't colored by the ill will you may feel toward your ex.

FROM PARTNER TO PLAYER

Occasionally, a broken man rises from the ashes of his breakup sporting a cool remove and studied cynicism, swearing off serious relationships in favor of an eternity of hookups. Though this man may seem like he's having fun, he's probably not happy. And while his transformation may look like growth, rest assured, it's mostly a regression.

Many people mistakenly believe that the goal of life is to be happy all the time. But happiness is short-lived. Joy is what our soul truly desires. Unfortunately, joy is only attainable through overcoming hardships, which gives us a real taste of our self-efficacy and resilience. So please don't become "that guy." The one who sates his soul with happiness because he's unwilling to do the work to experience joy. The one with a midlife crisis who splurges on a car he can't afford and courts women half his age. Save yourself the ridicule. I know I sound harsh here, but all of us have it in ourselves to heal and learn to love again. And hey, if dating multiple women casually at the same time is your thing, I'm not here to judge. But don't do it as a response to your hurt. Do it because that's what you authentically want.

The Right Moves

Most of what makes people jaded about dating is feeling like their efforts are getting them nowhere. But much like baking bread, there's a recipe for success in getting over someone and getting back out there. Sure, you can wing it. Some do, and it works. The question is: Do you want to hope for success, or do you want to create it? Now that we've got the wrong turns out of the way, we'll talk about a few specific steps you can take to move forward on the right track.

REEVALUATE WHAT YOU WANT

The dire mistake both men and women make after a breakup is not taking time to figure out what they want—by which I mean what they want that's similar to their prior relationship, and what they want that's completely different. Because what often happens is that we end up attracting people much like our disappointing ex. I say "we" because I've been guilty of walking out of one relationship right into an identical one. Ninety-five percent of our behavior is directed by our subconscious. If you don't keep yourself in check, it's easy to go back to your default—to what's familiar.

But in case you haven't noticed yet, that default is precisely what gets so many romantics into trouble. If it didn't work out with your ex, what makes you think choosing another woman like her is going to fare well? Take your time and reflect on what you do and don't want from your next relationship. Jot down traits your ex displayed that, in hindsight, should've been red flags; in another column, counter those traits with the kind you're looking for in someone new.

INVEST SLOWLY

Far too many men I work with go from zero to one hundred in the wake of a heartbreak, doubling down on their efforts without knowing if the woman deserves it. Like a poker player who's just gone all in only to lose everything, you might be overly eager to return to the table and win it all back. In your relatively fragile state, you might try to lose yourself in a new relationship as a means of relieving the pain from the last one. I'm not saying you should close yourself off to love altogether. But you need to learn to date wiser. After a breakup, it's usually hard to open yourself up and trust someone again. That's why it's more important now than ever to take your time to get to know the woman you're interested in, and only deepen a connection that feels worthwhile.

If you're the only one putting in as much effort as you are, then there's a problem. Only when she's reciprocating your efforts consistently should you invest more. Don't give her everything upfront. Take your time to make sure she's really the right person. Introduce her to your friends and get their opinion. Don't do all the initiating. Let her come to you, too. Listen not only to what she shares but to the meaning in between. Explore other options until you know she's worth it. That doesn't mean you have to lie to anyone. Simply put: take your time and invest slowly. This is how you date without getting hurt and better your chances of finding the right woman.

ASK THE RIGHT QUESTIONS

If there's anything my clients are tired of hearing me say, it's to ask more questions on dates. For those of you who work in sales, you understand the importance of questions in your work. Questions are an essential part of human communication. I'd argue that questions are the most valuable verbal communication tool we have. Why? Because questions help us learn about people without projecting our own ideas onto them. Questions open up worlds. When it comes to dating, questions are your best friend. If you take anything from this section, let it be this: the one asking the questions is the one in control of the conversation. So when you approach your dates inquisitively, you get to be in the driver's seat. You can learn what you need to about your date's likes, dislikes, values, and whatever else you need to know before jumping into a relationship. The reason this is relevant here is because after a breakup it's hard to trust again. I'm a huge advocate for doing whatever you can to minimize the risks of being hurt in dating. While I recognize that heartbreak and rejection are inevitable parts of the process, I also know that risk can be minimized. The more positive experiences you have on dates, the more likely you are to eventually end up in a healthy, loving relationship. I want that for you. So I highly encourage you to ask the important questions and learn about the women you're investing in before your emotions are completely entangled in the process.

Go Forth and Prosper

Takeaways

- Relationships aren't just about making us happy. They should help us grow. When you start looking at them that way, you can reframe your breakups and realize that losing someone is never truly a loss.
- Society teaches us to celebrate the beginning of love but not the ending of it. Be as respectful leaving a relationship as you were when entering it.
- Take your time before getting back out on the dating scene after a breakup. Focus on yourself and your healing. This is the best way to ensure that your efforts will be successful once you're ready to date again.

Action Items

- In a handful of words or simple phrases, write down the characteristics of a bad breakup you've experienced. Looking back, what could you have done differently?
- Reflect on moments in the past when you either over- or underinvested in someone you were dating. Knowing what you know now, how might you have handled the situation differently?

References

Anderson, Monica, Emily A. Vogels, and Erica Turner. "The Virtues and Downsides of Online Dating." Pew Research Center. February 6, 2020. Pewresearch.org/internet/2020/02/06/the-virtues-and -downsides-of-online-dating.

Davis, Clive M., Joani Blank, Hung-Yu Lin, and Consuelo Bonillas. "Characteristics of Vibrator Use among Women." *The Journal of Sex Research* 33, no. 4 (1996): 313–20. Accessed September 22, 2020. JSTOR.org/stable/3813277.

Lloyd, Elisabeth Anne. *The Case of the Female Orgasm: Bias in the Science of Evolution.* Cambridge, MA: Harvard University Press, 2005.

RAINN.org. "Victims of Sexual Violence: Statistics." Accessed September 22, 2020. RAINN.org/statistics/victims-sexual-violence.

Slangit. "Peacocking: What Does Peacocking Mean?" Accessed October 9, 2020. Slangit.com/meaning/peacocking.

Weisman, Carrie. "5 Things Women Wish Men Would Do in Bed More Often." *Fatherly.* Last modified January 28, 2021. Fatherly .com/love-money/what-women-want-men-to-do-in-bed-more.

Index

frequently asked
    questions, 63–64
planning, 62–63
securing future dates, 74–75
unsuccessful, 75–76
Flirting, 66–71
Friendships, 33, 127
Friend zone, 116, 120

G

Ghosting, 76, 127

H

Hart, Kevin, 17
Heartbreak, 131–132
Honesty, 11, 109, 128
"Hooking up," 106
Humor, 68–69

I

Ideal Partner Criteria, 42
Insecurity, 20–21. *See also*
    Jealousy
Integrity, 130–131
Intentional tension, 112–113
Intention-setting, 40–41
Intimacy. *See* Physical touch; Sex

J

Jealousy, 113–114

K

Kindness, vs. niceness, 8
Kissing, 63, 67–68, 86

L

Leading on, 108
Lifestyle, 33–34
Limiting beliefs, 20–21

M

Masculinity
    outdated notions of, 4–8
    positive traits, 9–15
Meeting women
    neighborhood locales, 50–51
    online, 51–55
    public social settings, 47
    sites of mutual interest, 48–49
    through friends, 43–44
    in the workplace, 45–46
#MeToo movement, 92
Milestones, 107, 117
Monroe, Marilyn, 68

N

Neediness, 118
Negging, 69
Niceness, vs. kindness, 8
No contact breakups, 130

Acknowledgments

First, I would like to thank my clients for investing in the process of working with me. They've given me the greatest gift of all: the opportunity to guide them and witness them excel in their romantic endeavors and beyond.

I must thank my parents, Rita and George, and my sisters, Mary, Christie, and Zoe for their unwavering love and support throughout this process. I would also like to thank my best friend Lydia for being a sounding board and for being the older sister I never had.

About the Author

Elsa Moreck is a certified dating, relationship, and social dynamics coach. She's empowered hundreds of people to be more courageous, conscious, and communicative in their dating lives so they can create meaningful relationships in an era when those are going extinct. Many of Elsa's clients have found loving relationships and have even had children with the partners that they met with her help. Furthermore, Elsa performs what she calls "organic matchmaking," which includes introducing men and women to each other in natural settings where they can intimately connect without the pressure of being set up on a date right off the bat. Elsa works with clients both one-on-one and in group settings. Her work has been featured in a multitude of places, including Tinder, Betches, *HuffPost*, and more. When she's not playing Hitch, Elsa loves learning foreign languages and enjoying novel experiences with her boyfriend and their dog. You can find her at ElsaMoreck.com.

CPSIA information can be obtained
at www.ICGtesting.com
Printed in the USA
JSHW021317020521
14195JS00001B/I